VOGUE KNITTING

BABY GIFTS

VOGUE KNITTING

BABY GIFTS

THE BUTTERICK® PUBLISHING COMPANY
NEW YORK

THE BUTTERICK® PUBLISHING COMPANY
161 Avenue of the Americas
New York, New York 10013

Library of Congress Cataloging-in-Publication Data

Vogue knitting baby gifts / [editor-in-chief, Trisha Malcolm].
    p. cm. – (Vogue knitting on the go!)
    ISBN 1-57389-027-8 (alk. paper)
    1. Knitting–Patterns. 2. Infants' clothing I. Title: Baby gifts. II. Malcolm, Trisha,
1960- III. Series.

TT825 .V59 2000
746.43'2043–dc21   00-064175

Manufactured in China

1 3 5 7 9 10 8 6 4 2

First Edition

TABLE OF CONTENTS

INTRODUCTION

Few gifts are more treasured than those made by hand, with love. When the recipient is someone as precious as a new baby, such gifts become keepsakes that are carefully saved or passed along through generations. Creating special baby gifts isn't as time-consuming as you might think, as this book will prove. Like all the projects in the *Knitting on the Go* series, these gifts were designed to be completed in spare moments, no matter where you might find them—on the bus, in a car, on the phone, or between appointments.

The projects in this book are as portable as they are adorable, and as delightful to create as they are to receive. They provide the perfect opportunity to try that new yarn, that new stitch, or that new technique. Or, if you wish, you can concoct a creation with quick, familiar stitches and yarn from your stash. The possibilities are endless!

Whatever your choice, the projects in this book are certain to warm more than the heart of the newest recipient on your gift list—the new baby in your life. Grab your needles now—babies don't stay babies for long—and get ready to **KNIT ON THE GO!**

THE BASICS

Handmade gifts have always been treasured keepsakes. For the knitter, the rewarding experience of creating a gift for a newborn provides a unique opportunity to explore and experiment with various stitches, techniques, and yarns, all on a small scale. A timeless Aran Baby Bunting (page 74) takes a new twist in a pale shade of lavender. Baby bibs are given a modern look in vibrant pastels (page 46), and the indispensable diaper bag sports a tailored Scottie dog motif (page 85).

This book is a celebration of creativity, design, and color for the new baby in your life. By marrying time-tested classics with present-day interpretation and the latest yarns, this collection of gifts offers comfort and style for today's baby. The variety of skill levels from novice to expert, the simple and concise instructions, and the portability of these sophisticated designs make this assortment of projects uniquely *Vogue Knitting on the go!*

SIZING

Most of the garments in this book are written for sizes 6 months through 24 months, with extra ease for your child to grow into the garment. You will notice a big jump in sleeve length from size 18 months to 24 months. The 24-month size is a transition from baby sizes to toddler sizes and as a result, will have a longer sleeve length.

Since children's measurements change so rapidly, it is best to measure your child or a sweater that fits well to determine which size to make.

YARN SELECTION

For an exact reproduction of the projects photographed, use the yarn listed in the "Materials" section of the pattern. We've chosen yarns that are readily available in the U.S. and Canada at the time of printing. The Resources list on pages 94 and 95 provides addresses of yarn distributors. Contact them for the name of a retailer in your area.

YARN SUBSTITUTION

You may wish to substitute yarns. Perhaps you view small-scale projects as a chance to incorporate leftovers from your yarn stash, or the yarn specified may not be available in your area. You'll need to knit to the given gauge to obtain the knitted measurements with a substitute yarn (see "Gauge" on page 11). Be sure to consider how the fiber content of the substitute yarn will affect the comfort and the ease of care of your projects.

To facilitate yarn substitution, *Vogue Knitting* grades yarn by the standard stitch gauge obtained in stockinette stitch. You'll find a grading number in the "Materials" section of the pattern, immediately following the fiber type of

GAUGE

It is always important to knit a gauge swatch, and it is even more so with garments to ensure proper fit.

Patterns usually state gauge over a 4"/10cm span; however, it's beneficial to make a larger test swatch. This gives a more precise stitch gauge, a better idea of the appearance and drape of the knitted fabric, and a chance for you to familiarize yourself with the stitch pattern.

The type of needles used—straight or double-pointed, wood or metal—will influence gauge, so knit your swatch with the needles you plan to use for the project. Measure gauge as illustrated. Try different needle sizes until your sample measures the required number of stitches and rows. *To get fewer stitches to the inch/cm, use larger needles; to get more stitches to the inch/cm, use smaller needles.*

Knitting in the round may tighten the gauge, so if you measured the gauge on a flat swatch, take another gauge reading after you begin knitting. When the piece measures at least 2"/5cm, lay it flat and measure over the stitches in the center of the piece, as the side stitches may be distorted.

It's a good idea to keep your gauge swatch in order to test blocking and cleaning methods.

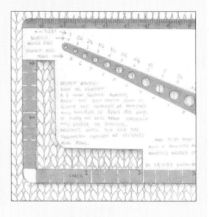

the yarn. Look for a substitute yarn that falls into the same category. The suggested needle size and gauge on the yarn label should be comparable to that on the "Yarn Symbols" chart (see page 16).

After you've successfully gauge-swatched a substitute yarn, you'll need to figure out how much of the substitute yarn the project requires. First, find the total length of the original yarn in the pattern (multiply number of balls by yards/meters per ball). Divide this figure by the new yards/meters per ball (listed on the yarn label). Round up to the next whole number. The answer is the number of balls required.

FOLLOWING CHARTS

Charts are a convenient way to follow colorwork, lace, cable, and other stitch patterns at a glance. *Vogue Knitting* stitch charts utilize the universal knitting language of "symbolcraft." When knitting back and forth in rows, read charts from right to left on right side (RS) rows and from left to right on wrong side (WS) rows, repeating any stitch and row repeats as directed in the pattern. When knitting in the round, read charts from right to left on every round. Posting a self-adhesive note under your working row is an easy way to keep track of your place on a chart.

LACE

Lace knitting provides a feminine touch. Knitted lace is formed with "yarn overs," which create an eyelet hole in combination with decreases that create directional effects. To make a yarn over (yo), merely pass the yarn over the right-hand needle to form a new loop. Decreases are worked as k2tog, ssk, or SKP depending on the desired slant and are spelled out specifically with each instruction. On the row or round that follows the lace or eyelet detail, each yarn over is treated as one stitch. If you're new to lace knitting, it's a good idea to count the stitches at the end of each row or round. Making a gauge swatch in the stitch pattern enables you to practice the lace pattern. Instead of binding off the swatch, place the final row on a holder, as the bind off tends to pull in the stitches and distort the gauge.

COLORWORK KNITTING

Two main types of colorwork are explored in this book: intarsia and stranding.

Intarsia

Intarsia is accomplished with separate bobbins of individual colors. This method is ideal for large blocks of color or for motifs that aren't repeated close together. When changing colors, always pick up the new color and wrap it around the old color to prevent holes.

For smaller areas of color, such as the accent diamonds on the Scottie Diaper Bag (page 85), work duplicate stitch embroidery after the pieces are knit.

Stranding

When motifs are closely placed, colorwork is accomplished by stranding along two or more colors per row, creating floats on the wrong side of the fabric. This technique is sometimes called Fair Isle knitting after the traditional Fair Isle patterns that are composed of small motifs with frequent color changes.

To keep an even tension and prevent holes while knitting, pick up yarns alternately over and under one another across or around. While knitting, stretch the stitches on the needle slightly wider than the length of the float at the back to keep work from puckering.

When changing colors at the beginning of rows or rounds, carry yarn along for a few rows only, or cut yarn and rejoin when needed. It is important to keep the floats small and neat so they don't catch on small fingers when the garment is pulled on.

BLOCKING

Blocking is a crucial finishing step in the knitting process. It is the best way to shape pattern pieces and smooth knitted edges in preparation for sewing together. Most garments retain their shape if the blocking

POMPOMS

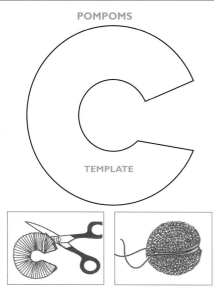

TEMPLATE

1 Following the template, cut two circular pieces of cardboard.

2 Hold the two circles together and wrap the yarn tightly around the cardboard several times. Secure and carefully cut the yarn.

3 Tie a piece of yarn tightly between the two circles. Remove the cardboard and trim the pompom to the desired size.

EMBROIDERY STITCHES

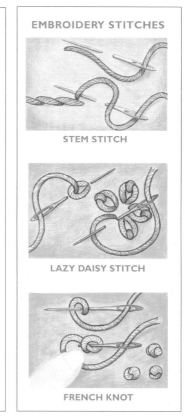

STEM STITCH

LAZY DAISY STITCH

FRENCH KNOT

DUPLICATE STITCH

Duplicate stitch covers a knit stitch. Bring the needle up below the stitch to be worked. Insert the needle under both loops one row above and pull it through. Insert it back into the stitch below and through the center of the next stitch in one motion, as shown.

stages in the instructions are followed carefully. Choose a blocking method according to the instructions on the yarn care label, and when in doubt, test-block your gauge swatch.

Wet Block Method

Using rust-proof pins, pin pieces to measurements on a flat surface and lightly dampen using a spray bottle. Allow to dry before removing pins.

Steam Block Method

With wrong sides facing, pin pieces. Steam lightly, holding the iron 2"/5cm above the knitting. Do not press or it will flatten stitches.

FINISHING

The pieces in this book use a variety of finishing techniques, from crocheting around the edges to embroidery on the collar. Also refer to the illustrations provided for other useful techniques: knitting with double-pointed needles, joining in the round, and embroidery stitches.

CARE

Refer to the yarn label for the recommended cleaning method. Many of the projects in the book can be either washed by hand, or in the machine on a gentle or wool cycle, using lukewarm water with a mild detergent. Do not agitate or soak for more than 10 minutes. Rinse gently with tepid water, then fold in a towel and gently press the water out. Lay flat to dry, away from excess heat and light. Check the yarn label for any specific care instructions such as dry cleaning or tumble drying.

JOINING ROUNDS

DOUBLE-POINTED NEEDLES

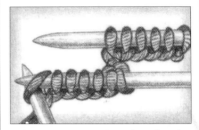

I Cast on the required number of stitches on the first needle, plus one extra. Slip this extra stitch to the next needle as shown. Continue in this way, casting on the required number of stitches on the last needle.

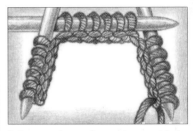

2 Arrange the needles as shown, with the cast-on edge facing the center of the triangle (or square).

3 Place a stitch marker after the last cast-on stitch. With the free needle, knit the first cast-on stitch, pulling the yarn tightly. Continue knitting in rounds, slipping the marker before beginning each round.

CIRCULAR NEEDLES

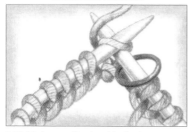

I Hold the needle tip with the last cast-on stitch in your right hand and the tip with the first cast-on stitch in your left hand. Knit the first cast-on stitch, pulling the yarn tight to avoid a gap.

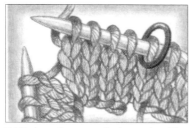

2 Work until you reach the marker. This completes the first round. Slip the marker to the right needle and work the next round.

TWISTED CORD

I If you have someone to help you, insert a pencil or knitting needle through each end of the strands. If not, place one end over a doorknob and put a pencil through the other end. Turn the strands clockwise until they are tightly twisted.

2 Keeping the strands taut, fold the piece in half. Remove the pencils and allow the cords to twist onto themselves.

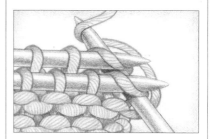

I With RS placed together, hold pieces on two parallel needles. Insert a third needle knitwise into the first stitch of each needle, and wrap the yarn around the needle as if to knit.

2 Knit these two stitches together, and slip them off the needles. *Knit the next two stitches together in the same manner.

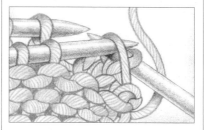

3 Slip the first stitch on the third needle over the second stitch and off the needle. Repeat from the * in Step 2 across the row until all stitches have been bound off.

KNITTING TERMS AND ABBREVIATIONS

approx approximately

beg begin(ning)

bind off Used to finish an edge and keep stitches from unraveling. Lift the first stitch over the second, the second over the third, etc. (UK: cast off)

cast on A foundation row of stitches placed on the needle in order to begin knitting.

CC contrast color

ch chain(s)

cm centimeter(s)

cont continu(e)(ing)

dc double crochet (UK: tr–treble)

dec decrease(ing)–Reduce the stitches in a row (knit 2 together).

dpn double-pointed needle(s)

foll follow(s)(ing)

g gram(s)

garter stitch Knit every row. Circular knitting: knit one round, then purl one round.

hdc half double crochet (UK: htr–half treble)

inc increase(ing)–Add stitches in a row (knit into the front and back of a stitch).

k knit

k2tog knit 2 stitches together

LH left-hand

lp(s) loop(s)

m meter(s)

M1 make one stitch–With the needle tip, lift the strand between last stitch worked and next stitch on the left-hand needle and knit into the back of it. One stitch has been added.

YARN SYMBOLS

① **Fine Weight**
(29-32 stitches per 4"/10cm)
Includes baby and fingering yarns, and some of the heavier crochet cottons. The range of needle sizes is 0-4 (2-3.5mm).

② **Lightweight**
(25-28 stitches per 4"/10cm)
Includes sport yarn, sock yarn, UK 4-ply, and lightweight DK yarns. The range of needle sizes is 3-6 (3.25-4mm).

③ **Medium Weight**
(21-24 stitches per 4"/10cm)
Includes DK and worsted, the most commonly used knitting yarns. The range of needle sizes is 6-9 (4-5.5mm).

④ **Medium-heavy Weight**
(17-20 stitches per 4"/10cm)
Also called heavy worsted or Aran. The range of needle sizes is 8-10 (5-6mm).

⑤ **Bulky Weight**
(13-16 stitches per 4"/10cm)
Also called chunky. Includes heavier Icelandic yarns. The range of needle sizes is 10-11 (6-8mm).

⑥ **Extra-bulky Weight**
(9-12 stitches per 4"/10cm)
The heaviest yarns available. The range of needle sizes is 11 and up (8mm and up).

MC main color

mm millimeter(s)

no stitch On some charts, "no stitch" is indicated with shaded spaces where stitches have been decreased or not yet made. In such cases, work the stitches of the chart, skipping over the "no stitch" spaces.

oz ounce(s)

p purl

p2tog purl 2 stitches together

pat(s) pattern

pick up and knit (purl) Knit (or purl) into the loops along an edge.

pm place markers–Place or attach a loop of contrast yarn or purchased stitch marker as indicated.

psso pass slip stitch(es) over

rem remain(s)(ing)

rep repeat

rev St st reverse Stockinette stitch–Purl right-side rows, knit wrong-side rows. Circular knitting: purl all rounds. (UK: reverse stocking stitch)

rnd(s) round(s)

RH right-hand

RS right side(s)

sc single crochet (UK: dc–double crochet)

sk skip

SKP Slip 1, knit 1, pass slip stitch over knit 1.

SK2P Slip 1, knit 2 together, pass slip stitch over the knit 2 together.

sl slip–An unworked stitch made by passing a stitch from the left-hand to the right-hand needle as if to purl.

sl st slip stitch (UK: sc–single crochet)

ssk slip, slip, knit–Slip next 2 stitches knitwise, one at a time, to right-hand needle. Insert tip of left-hand needle into fronts of these stitches from left to right. Knit them together. One stitch has been decreased.

sssk Slip next 3 sts knitwise, one at a time, to right-hand needle. Insert tip of left-hand needle into fronts of these stitches from left to right. Knit them together. Two stitches have been decreased.

st(s) stitch(es)

St st Stockinette stitch–Knit right-side rows, purl wrong-side rows. Circular knitting: knit all rounds. (UK: stocking stitch)

tbl through back of loop

tog together

WS wrong side(s)

wyib with yarn in back

wyif with yarn in front

work even Continue in pattern without increasing or decreasing. (UK: work straight)

yd yard(s)

yo yarn over–Make a new stitch by wrapping the yarn over the right-hand needle. (UK: yfwd, yon, yrn)

* = Repeat directions following * as many times as indicated.

[ ] = Repeat directions inside brackets as many times as indicated.

PATCHWORK PULLOVER

Flower patch

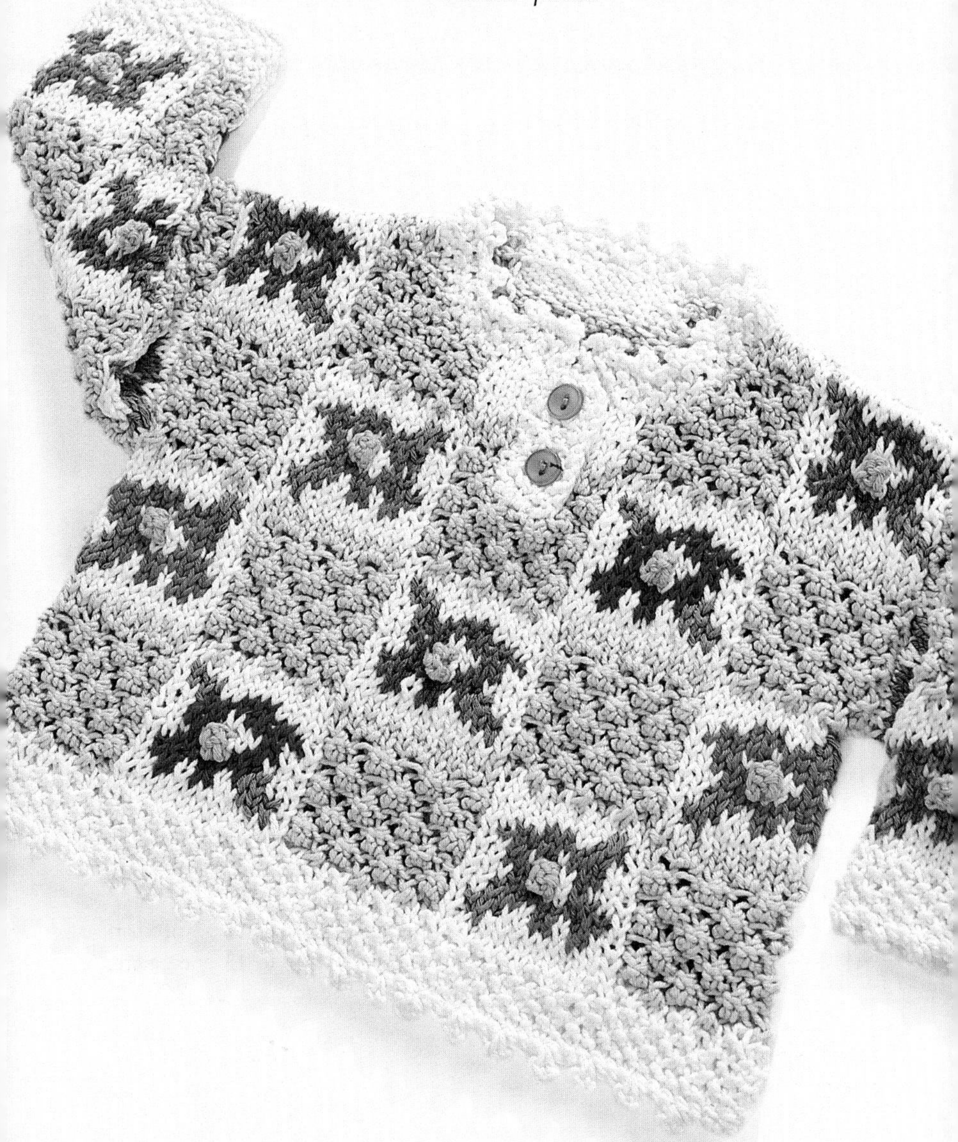

Sasha Kagan designed this floral and patchwork blackberry-stitch pullover to keep baby warm on cool spring days. Delicate crochet picot edges continue the theme of texture. Bobbles are knit separately, then sewn to the center of the flowers.

SIZES

Instructions are written for size 3-6 months.

KNITTED MEASUREMENTS

▨ Chest 20"/51cm
▨ Length 9½"/24cm
▨ Upper arm 8"/20.5cm

MATERIALS

▨ 2 1¾oz/50g balls (each approx 127yd/115m) of Rowan *Cotton Glace* (cotton③) each in #726 white (A) and #722 pale green (B)
▨ 1 ball each in #795 butter (C), #724 pink (D) and #748 green (E)
▨ 1 1¾oz/50g balls (each approx 187yd/170m) of Rowan *4 Ply Cotton* (cotton③) each in #104 purple (F), #114 periwinkle (G) and #106 magenta (H)
▨ One pair each sizes 3 and 5 (3mm and 3.75mm) needles *or size to obtain gauge*
▨ Crochet hook size B/1 (2mm)
▨ Two ½"/12mm buttons
▨ Stitch markers
▨ Stitch holders

GAUGE

26 sts and 28 rows to 4"/10cm over pat st using larger needles

Take time to check gauge.

STITCH GLOSSARY

Blackberry Stitch

(over 13 sts)
Row 1 (RS) Knit.
Row 2 *[K1, p1, k1] into next st, p3tog; rep from * to last st, [k1, p1, k1] into last st—15 sts.
Row 3 Purl.
Row 4 *P3tog, [k1, p1, k1] into next st; rep from * to last 3 sts, p3tog—13 sts.
Row 5 Purl.
Rows 6-9 Rep rows 2-5.
Rows 10-12 Rep rows 2-4.
Row 13 Knit.

Seed Stitch

Row 1 (RS) K1, *p1, k1; rep from * to end.
Row 2 K the purl sts and p the knit sts.
Rep row 2 for seed st.

MB (Make Bobble)
K into back and front of st, turn; k2, turn; p2, turn; k2, turn; k2tog. Cut yarn, leaving an end for sewing.

BACK

With smaller needles and A, cast on 65 sts. Work in seed st for 6 rows. Change to larger needles.

Beg chart pat

Row 1 (RS) Work sts 1 to 52 of chart once, then work sts 1 to 13 once more. Cont as established through row 56.

Shoulder shaping

With A, bind off 9 sts at beg of next 4 rows. Leave rem 29 sts on holder for back neck.

FRONT

With smaller needles and A, cast on 65 sts. Work in seed st for 6 rows. Change to larger needles.

Beg chart pat

Row 1 (RS) Work sts 14 to 52 of chart once, then work sts 1 to 26 once. Cont as established through row 34.

Neck shaping

Next row (RS) Cont in chart pat, work 30 sts, join 2nd ball of yarn and bind off center 5 sts, work to end. Working both sides at once, work even for 11 more rows.

Next row (RS) (row 47 of chart) Work to last 5 sts of left front, slip these 5 sts to holder, work first 5 sts of right front, slip these 5 sts to holder, work to end. Dec 1 st at each neck edge *every* row 7 times. Work even to end of chart, and when same length as back to shoulders, shape shoulders as for back.

RIGHT SLEEVE

With smaller needles and A, cast on 35 sts. Work in seed st for 6 rows, inc 1 st on last row—36 sts. Change to larger needles.

Beg chart pat

Row 1 (RS) Work sts 9-44 of chart. Cont as established through row 41, AT SAME TIME, inc 1 st each side every 4th row 6 times, every 6th row twice—52 sts. Work even to end of chart. With A, bind off on WS.

LEFT SLEEVE

Cast on and work seed st as for right sleeve. Change to larger needles.

Beg chart pat

Row 1 (RS) Work sts 22 to 52 of chart once, then sts 1 to 5 once. Complete as for right sleeve.

FINISHING

Block pieces to measurements. Make bobbles and sew on where indicated on chart.

Buttonband

With RS facing, smaller needles and A, pick up and k 11 sts along left front straight neck opening. Work in seed st for 6 rows. Bind off in pat.

Buttonhole band

With RS facing, smaller needles and A, pick up and k 11 sts along right front straight neck opening. Work in seed st for 3 rows.

Next (buttonhole) row (RS) Work 2 sts, bind off 2 sts, work 3 sts, bind off 2 sts, work 2 sts. On next row, cast on 2 sts over bound off sts. Work 1 row more. Bind off in pat.

Sew button band and buttonhole band edges to front neck opening. Sew shoulder seams.

Neckband

With RS facing, smaller needles and A, beg at center of buttonhole band edge, pick up and k 3 sts along buttonhole band, k across 5 sts from holder, pick up and k 14 sts along front neck, k across 29 sts from back neck holder, pick up and k 14 sts along right front, k 5 sts from holder, pick up and k 3 sts over first half of buttonband edge—73 sts. Work in seed st for 3 rows. Bind off in pat.

Place markers 4"/10cm down from shoulders on front and back. Sew sleeves between markers. Sew side and sleeve seams. Sew on buttons opposite buttonholes.

Picot edging

With WS facing, crochet hook and A, beg at left front neckband edge, work 1 ch into into last bind-off st, *1 sc in next st, ch 3, 1 sc in same st, sc in next 3 sts; rep from * around.

Work picot edging around cast-on edges of body and sleeves.

Press edging lightly if required.

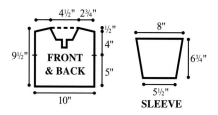

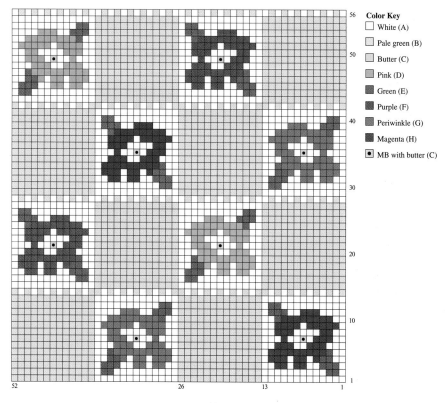

56
50
40
30
20
10
1

Color Key
- ☐ White (A)
- ☐ Pale green (B)
- ☐ Butter (C)
- ☐ Pink (D)
- ☐ Green (E)
- ☐ Purple (F)
- ☐ Periwinkle (G)
- ☐ Magenta (H)
- ⊡ MB with butter (C)

52   26   13   1

Toboggan twosome

Lipp Holmfeld's helmet and matching mittens are designed to keep little heads and hands toasty warm in the winter. Stockinette stitch on the mitten palms and thumbs creates a smooth contrast to the textural seed-stich top.

SIZE

▓ Helmet fits head sizes 15" to 18"/38cm to 45.5cm

▓ Mittens fit 1 to 2 years

MATERIALS

▓ 2 1¾oz/50b balls (each approx 219yd/ 203m of Lang/Berroco, Inc. *Bébé Lang* (wool ②) in #7106 blue

▓ One pair size 4 (3.5mm) needles *or size to obtain gauge*

▓ One set (4) size 4 (3.5mm) dpn

▓ Stitch holder and marker

GAUGE

22 sts and 40 rows to 4"/10cm over seed st using size 4 (3.5mm) needles.
Take time to check gauge.

STITCH GLOSSARY

Seed Stitch
Row 1 (RS) *K1, p1; rep from * to end.
Row 2 K the purl sts and p the knit sts.
Rep row 2 for seed st.

HELMET

With single-pointed needles, cast on 1 st for beg of one ear flap.
Row 1 (RS) [K1, p1, k1] in 1 st—3 sts.
Row 2 K1, p1, [k1, p1] in last st—4 sts.
Row 3 P1, k1, p1, [k1, p1] in last st—5 sts.
Cont in seed st, inc 1 st at end of every row, until there are 28 sts. Cut yarn. Place sts on a holder.
Make a 2nd earflap in same way, do *not* cut yarn.
Join ear flaps
Next row (RS) Work seed st over 28 sts of 2nd flap, with RS of sts on holder facing, cont seed st over 28 sts from holder, inc 1 st in last st—57 sts. Cont in seed st, inc 1 st at end of every row until there are 70 sts. **Next row** Cast on 11 sts, work to end—81 sts. Divide sts over 3 dpn (27 sts on each needle). Join, place marker for end of rnd and sl marker every rnd. Cont in seed st for 18 rnds.
Top shaping
Rnd 1 *Work 25 sts, k2tog; rep from * around—78 sts.
Rnds 2 and 3 *Work 25 sts in seed st, k1; rep from * around.
Rnd 4 *Work 11 sts, k2tog; rep from * around—72 sts.
Rnds 5 and 6 *Work 11 sts in seed st, k1; rep from * around.
Rnd 7 *Work 10 sts, k2tog; rep from * around—66 sts.
Rnds 5 and 6 *Work 10 sts in seed st, k1; rep from * around.

Cont in this way to dec 6 sts every 3rd rnd, working 1 less st between decs every dec rnd and keeping k st as established, until there are 12 sts (4 sts on each needle).

Next rnd [K2tog] 6 times. Cut yarn and draw through rem 6 sts.

FINISHING

Block piece. Make a 2"/5cm pompom and sew to top of hat. With two strands held tog, make two twisted cords each approx 6½"/16.5cm long (finished length) and sew to end of each earflap.

MITTENS

RIGHT HAND

With dpn, cast on 30 sts. Divide sts over 3 needles as foll: *Needle 1* 17 sts; *Needle 2* 7 sts; *Needle 3* 6 sts. Join, taking care not to twist sts on needle. Place marker for end of rnd and sl marker every rnd. Work in k1, p1 rib for 12 rnds.

Next 11 rnds Work17 sts in seed st, work 13 sts in St st.

Next rnd Work 17 sts seed st, using a 12"/30.5cm length of a contrasting color yarn, k5 (thumb sts), sl these 5 sts back to LH needle and with main yarn k them again. Work even in pats for 10 rnds.

Top shaping

Rnd 1 SKP, work 13 sts seed st, k2tog, SKP, k9, k2tog. Place inside hand sts on one needle.

Rnd 2 K1, work 13 sts seed st, k1, k to end.

Rnd 3 SKP, work 11 sts seed st, k2tog, SKP, k7, k2tog.

Rnd 4 K1, work 11 sts seed st, k1, k to end. Cont in this way to dec 2 sts every other rnd until there are 10 sts— 7 sts on *Needle 1* and 3 sts on *Needle 2*. K2tog 5 times, cut yarn and draw through rem sts.

THUMB

Pull out contrasting yarn. There are 5 loops on top and 5 loops on bottom. Sl 5 top loops to one dpn and pick up 1 st in corner, sl 5 bottom loops to 2nd dpn and pick up 1 st in corner—6 sts on each of two needles. Join and work in St st for 12 rnds. K2tog 6 times, then cut yarn and draw through rem sts.

RECEIVING BLANKET
Pastel dominoes

A garter stitch, mosaic pattern adds extra warmth and texture to this charming coverlet. Its pastel colors suit both sexes, making it the perfect wrap for carrying baby home from the hospital. Designed by Barbara Venishnick.

▓ 22" x 27"/56cm x 68.5cm

▓ 4 1¾oz/50g balls (each approx 117yd/106m of Naturally/S.R. Kertzer Ltd. *Cotton Candy DK in* #504 natural (MC)
▓ 2 balls each in #503 blue (A), #502 pink (B) and #501 green (C)
▓ Size 6 (4mm) circular needles 32"/81cm long or *size to obtain gauge*

24 sts and 45 rows to 4"/10cm over mosaic pat using size 6 (4mm) needles. *Take time to check gauge.*

Notes
1 Sl all sts purlwise.
2 On RS rows, work all slipped sts with yarn in back. On WS rows, work all slipped sts with yarn in front.
3 Always knit the first and last st of every row, matching contrasting color, for selvage sts.

MOSAIC PATTERN
(multiple of 14 sts)
Row 1 With A, k7, [sl 1, k1] 3 times, sl 1.
Row 2 With A, [sl 1, k1] 3 times, sl 1, k7.
Row 3 With MC, [sl 1, k1] 3 times, sl 1, k7.
Row 4 With MC, k7, [sl 1, k1] 3 times, sl 1.
Rows 5-12 Rep rows 1-4 twice.
Rows 13 and 14 Rep rows 1 and 2 once.
Rows 15 and 16 With MC, knit.
Row 17 With A, [sl 1, k1] 3 times, sl 1, k7.
Row 18 With A, k7, [sl 1, k1] 3 times, sl 1.
Row 19 With MC, k7, [sl 1, k1] 3 times, sl 1.
Row 20 With MC, [sl 1, k1] 3 times, sl 1, k7.
Rows 21-28 Rep rows 17-20 twice.
Rows 29 and 30 Rep rows 17 and 18.
Rows 31 and 32 With MC, knit.
Rep rows 1-32 for mosaic pat.

With MC, cast on 128 sts.
Beg mosaic pat
Row 1 (RS) *With A, k1 (selvage st), work 14 sts in mosaic pat, with B work 14 sts mosaic pat, with C work 14 sts mosaic pat; rep from * twice more, end with k1 in color C (selvage st). Cont as established until 32 rows of pat have worked. Shift all colors to the left as indicated on the color placement chart.
Hint
Do not cut yarn, carry the color along the back of the blanket, twisting it along with MC on row 31 to its new position. Only the last color of the row will have to be cut. This greatly reduces the ends to be

woven in and makes for a neater and more durable blanket. Cont to foll mosaic pat and color placement chart. End last rep with row 31. Do *not* turn.

TRIM

With MC still attached and with RS facing, pm for corner, pick up 163 sts along the left side of blanket, pm for corner, pick up 128 sts along the cast-on edge, pm for corner, pick up 163 sts along right side of blanket, pm for corner, pick up 128 sts along the bound-off edge, pm for corner and beg of rnd—582 sts. Join and work in rnds as foll: P 1 rnd. K around, inc 1 st on each side of each corner marker—590 sts. P 1 rnd. K around, inc 1 st on each side of each corner marker—598 sts. P 1 rnd. K around, inc 1 st on each side of each corner marker—606 sts. Bind off all sts purlwise. Weave in all ends.

A	C	B	A	C	B	A	C	B
B	A	C	B	A	C	B	A	C
C	B	A	C	B	A	C	B	A
A	C	B	A	C	B	A	C	B
B	A	C	B	A	C	B	A	C
C	B	A	C	B	A	C	B	A
A	C	B	A	C	B	A	C	B
B	A	C	B	A	C	B	A	C
C	B	A	C	B	A	C	B	A

A Blue

B Pink

C Green

SAILOR SWEATER

Anchors aweigh!

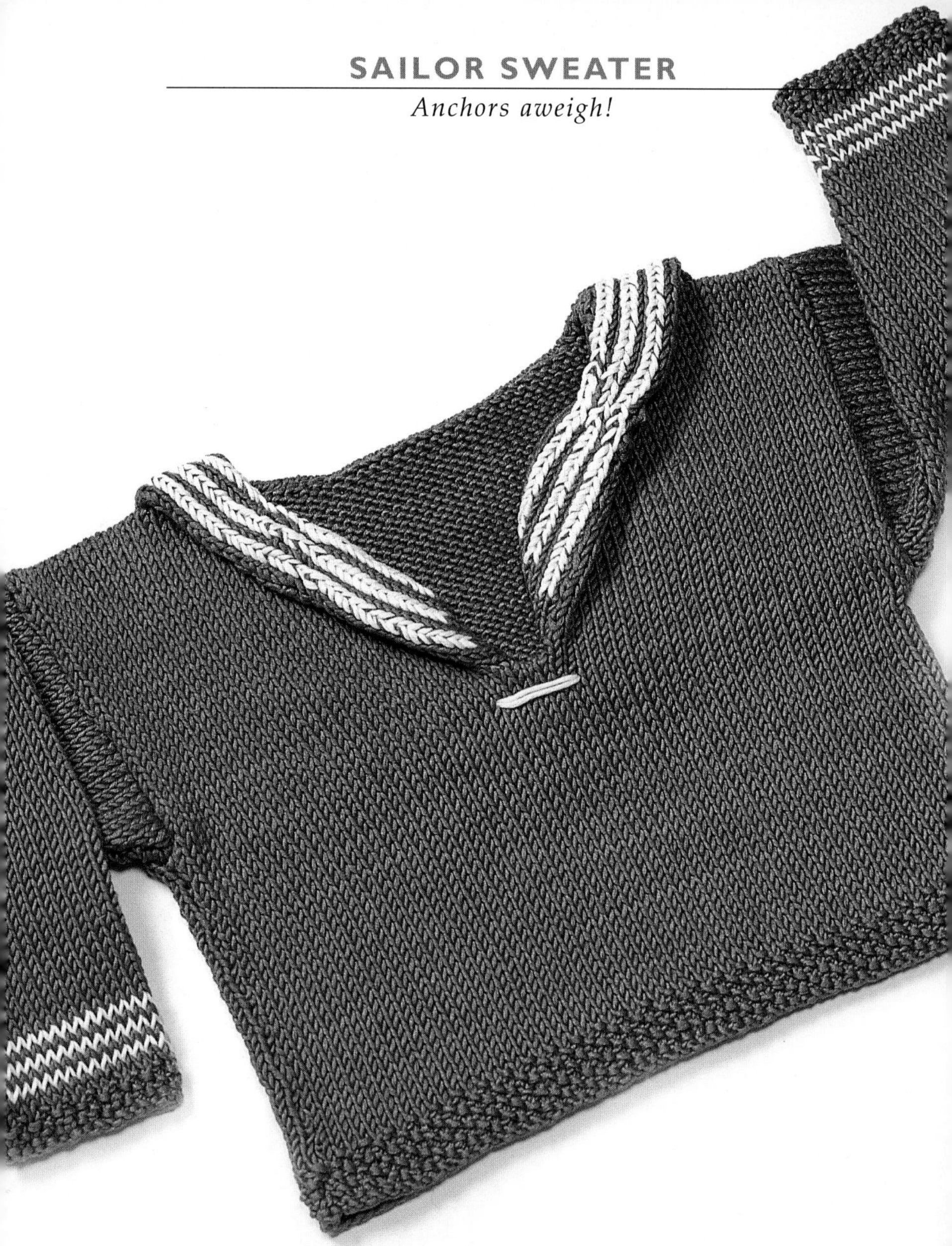

For Intermediate Knitters

Your little skipper can sail the seven seas in this nautical pullover designed by Besty Westman. Knit-in stripes at the cuff and around the collar replicate traditional navy wear.

SIZES

Instructions are written for size 6 months. Changes for sizes 12, 18 and 24 months are in parentheses.

KNITTED MEASUREMENTS

▨ Chest 22 (23, 24, 26)"/56 (58.5, 61, 66)cm
▨ Length 10 (11, 12, 14)"/25.5 (28, 30.5, 35.5)cm
▨ Upper arm 10 (10½, 11, 11½)"/25.5 (26.5, 28, 29)cm

MATERIALS

▨ 4 (5, 5, 6) 1¾oz/50g balls (each approx 114yd/105m) of Dale of Norway *Kolibri* (cotton③) in #5836 blue (MC)
▨ 1 ball in #0010 white (CC)
▨ One pair each sizes 3 and 4 (3mm and 3.5mm) needles *or size to obtain gauge*
▨ Two ⅝"/15mm buttons
▨ Stitch markers

GAUGE

24 sts and 30 rows to 4"/10cm over St st using size 4 (3.5mm) needles.
Take time to check gauge.

STITCH GLOSSARY

Seed Stitch
Row 1 (RS) K1, *p1, k1; rep from * to end.
Row 2 P the knit sts and k the purl sts.
Rep row 2 for seed st.

BACK

With smaller needles and MC, cast on 65 (69, 73, 79) sts. Work in seed st for 8 (8, 10, 10) rows. Change to larger needles and work in St st until piece measures 9½ (10½, 11½ 13½)"/24 (26.5, 29, 34)cm from beg, end with a WS row.
Neck shaping
Next row (RS) K 25 (27, 28, 31) sts, join 2nd ball of yarn and bind off center 15 (15, 17, 17) sts, k to end. Working both sides at once, bind off 6 (7, 7, 8) sts from each neck once. Work 1 row even. Bind off rem 19 (20, 21, 23) sts each side for shoulders.

FRONT

Work as for back until piece measures 6 (6½, 7, 8½)"/15 (16.5, 18, 21.5)cm from beg, end with a WS row.
Neck shaping
Next row (RS) Work 32 (34, 36, 39) sts, join 2nd ball of yarn and bind off center st, work to end. Working both sides at once, cont even for 2¼ (2½, 3, 3¼)"/5.5 (6.5, 7.5, 8)cm. Place a marker at each neck edge. Dec 1 st at each neck edge *every* row 13 (14, 15, 16) times. Bind off rem 19 (20, 21, 23) sts each side for shoulders.

SLEEVES

With smaller needles and MC, cast on 37 (39, 41, 43) sts. Work in seed st for 5 (5, 7, 7) rows. Change to larger needles. Cont in St st (beg with a p row on WS) work [1 row MC, 1 row CC] 3 times, then cont in MC, AT SAME TIME, inc 1 st each side every 2nd (2nd, 2nd, 4th) row 7 (4, 1, 4) times, every 4th (4th, 4th, 6th) row 5 (8, 11, 9) times—61 (63, 65, 69) sts. Work even until piece measures 6 (6¾, 7¾, 11)"/15 (17, 19.5, 28)cm from beg. Bind off.

FINISHING

Block pieces to measurements.
Sew shoulder seams.

Collar

With smaller needles and MC, cast on 55 (57, 63, 65) sts.

Rows 1 and 2 Purl.

Row 3 (RS) K2 MC, k with CC to last 2 sts, k2 MC.

Row 4 P2 MC, p1 CC, p with MC to last 3 sts, join 2nd ball of CC and p1, k2 MC.

Row 5 K2 MC, k1 CC, k1 MC, k with CC to last 4 sts, k1 MC, k1 CC, k2 MC.

Row 6 P2 MC, p1 CC, p1 MC, p1 CC, p with MC to last 5 sts, p1 CC, p1 MC, p1 CC, p2 MC.

Row 7 K2 MC, [k1 CC, k1 MC] twice, k with CC to last 6 sts, [k1 MC, k1 CC] twice, k2 MC.

Row 8 P2 MC, [p1 CC, p1 MC] twice, p1 CC, p with MC to last 7 sts, [p1 CC, p1 MC] twice, p1 CC, p2 MC.

Row 9 K2 MC, [k1 CC, k1 MC] twice, k1 CC, k with MC to last 7 sts, [k1 CC, k1 MC] twice, k1 CC, k2 MC.

Rep last 2 rows until collar measures 5 (5¼, 5½, 5¾)"/12.5 (13, 14, 14.5)cm from beg, end with a WS row.

Neck shaping

Keeping CC sts as established, work 20 (21, 23, 24) sts, join 2nd ball of MC, bind off center 15 (15, 17, 17) sts, work to end. Working both sides at once, bind off 6 (7, 8, 9) sts from each neck once, then dec 1 st at each neck edge every other row 7 (7, 8, 8) times—7 sts.

Work over rem 7 sts each side for 2 rows, place marker at each outer edge. Work 2¼ (2½, 3, 3¼)"/5.5 (6.5, 7.5, 8)cm more, end with a WS row.

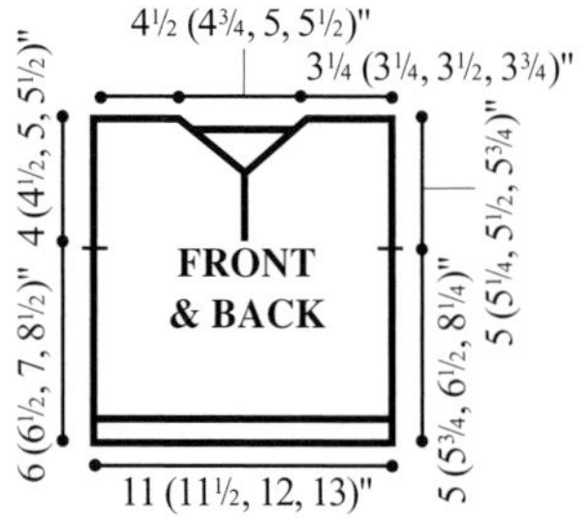
4½ (4¾, 5, 5½)"
3¼ (3¼, 3½, 3¾)"
4 (4½, 5, 5½)"
6 (6½, 7, 8½)"
FRONT
& BACK
5 (5¼, 5½, 5¾)"
5 (5¾, 6½, 8¼)"
11 (11½, 12, 13)"

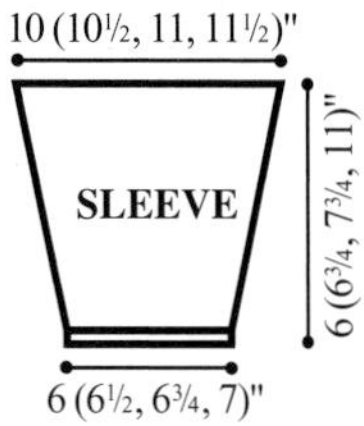
10 (10½, 11, 11½)"
SLEEVE
6 (6¾, 7¾, 11)"
6 (6½, 6¾, 7)"

Facing

Next row (RS) Work 7 sts from first needle, do *not* turn, cast on 3 sts, work 7 sts from 2nd needle—17 sts. With MC only, work even in St st for 7 rows. K 2 rows. Bind off knitwise on WS. Block collar. With right sides tog, sew facing to straight front neck opening until markers meet, then with WS of sweater and RS of collar tog, sew collar in place.

Place markers 5 (5¼, 5½, 5¾)"/13 (13.5, 14, 14.5)cm down from shoulder seams on front and back for armholes. Sew top of sleeves between markers. Sew side and sleeve seams.

Sew one button each into MC corners of collar. With 2 strands of MC and tapestry needle make 1 horizontal stitch across the center front 7 sts ½"/1.5cm down from front neck opening.

LACE BODICE DRESS
Party frock

A knitted shell pattern borders the neck, sleeves, and bottom edge of this sweet lace bodice. It is made with a cloud-soft cashmere/silk blend. Attach a silky skirt to make a dress that will turn your little one into a princess. Designed by Veronica Manno.

SIZES

Instructions are written for size 6 months. Changes for sizes 12, 18, and 24 months are in parentheses.

KNITTED MEASUREMENTS

▒ Chest 21 (23, 25, 27)"/53.5 (58.5, 63.5, 68.5)cm

▒ Upper arm 6½ (6½, 7½, 7½)"/16.5 (16.5, 19, 19)cm

MATERIALS

▒ 1 (1, 2, 2) 1¾oz/50g hanks (each approx 228yd/208m) of Cherry Tree Hill Yarn *Cashmere and Silk 2 ply* (cashmere/silk③) in "Mother of Pearl" pink

▒ One pair size 3 (3mm) needles *or size to obtain gauge*

▒ Crochet hook size D/3 (3mm)

▒ One ⅜"/10mm button

▒ ½ (¾, 1, 1)yd/.5 (.75, 1, 1)m silk fabric 45"/114cm wide

Silk charmeuse by Exotic Silks
252 State Street
Los Altos, CA 94022

▒ Matching sewing thread

▒ Stitch markers

GAUGE

24 sts and 36 rows to 4"/10cm over eyelet pat using size 3 (3mm) needles.
Take time to check gauge.

STITCH GLOSSARY

Scalloped Shell Edging
(multiple of 11 sts plus 2)
Foundation row (WS) Purl.
Row 1 (RS) K2, *k1, slip this st back to LH needle and slip the next 8 sts over this st and off needle, [yo] twice, then k the first st again, k2; rep from * to end.
Row 2 P1, *p2tog, drop 1 yo, [p1, p1tbl] twice into 2nd yo, p1; rep from * to last st, p1.
Rows 3 and 4 Knit.

Eyelet Pattern
(multiple of 6 sts plus 3)
Rows 1 and 3 (RS) Knit.
Row 2 and all WS rows Purl.
Row 5 *K4, yo, ssk; rep from * to last 3 sts, k3.
Row 7 K1, *k1, k2tog, yo, k1, yo, ssk; rep from * to last 2 sts, k2.
Rows 9 and 11 Knit.
Row 13 *K1, yo, ssk, k3; rep from * to last 3 sts, k1, yo, ssk.
Row 15 K1, *k1, yo ssk, k1, k2tog, yo; rep from * to last 2 sts, k2.
Row 16 Purl.
Rep rows 1-6 for eyelet pat.

BODICE FRONT

Cast on 112 (123, 134, 145) sts. Work rows 1-4 of scalloped shell edging—62 (68, 74, 80) sts.

Beg eyelet pat

Next row (RS) Work row 1 of eyelet pat, inc 1 st—63 (69, 75, 81) sts. Cont in eyelet pat for 2 (2½, 3, 3¾)"/5 (6.5, 7.5, 9.5)cm, end with a WS row.

Armhole shaping

Bind off 3 sts at beg next 2 rows, 2 sts at beg of next 2 rows, dec 1 st each side every other row twice—49 (55, 61, 67) sts. Work even until armhole measures 1½ (1¾, 2, 2½)"/3.5 (4.5, 5, 6)cm, end with a WS row.

Neck shaping

Next row Work 20 (22, 25, 27) sts, join 2nd ball of yarn and bind off center 9 (11, 11, 13) sts, work to end. Working both sides at once, bind off from each neck edge 3 sts once, 2 sts once, dec 1 st every other row 3 times. Work even until armhole measures 3 (3¼, 3½, 4)"/7.5 (8.5, 9, 10)cm. Bind off rem 12 (14, 17, 19) sts each side for shoulders.

BACK

Work as for front until armhole measures 1¼ (1¼, 1½, 1½)"/3 (3, 4, 4) cm, end with a WS row.

Placket shaping

Next row (RS) Work 24 (27, 30, 33) sts, join 2nd ball of yarn and k2tog, work to end. Work both sides at once until same length as front to shoulders. Bind off all sts each side. Place a marker 12 (14, 17, 19) sts in from each shoulder edge.

SLEEVES

Cast on 68 (68, 79, 79) sts. Work rows 1-4 of scalloped shell edging—38 (38, 44, 44) sts.

Beg eyelet pat

Next row (RS) Work row 1 of eyelet pat, inc 1 st—39 (39, 45, 45) sts. Cont in eyelet pat for 1 (1¼, 1½, 1½)"/2.5 (3, 4, 4) cm, end with a WS row.

Cap shaping

Bind off 3 sts at beg next 2 rows, 2 sts at beg of next 2 rows, dec 1 st each side every other row 6 (6, 8, 8) times. Bind off 3 sts beg next 2 rows. Bind off rem 11 (11, 13, 13) sts.

FINISHING

Collar

Cast on 112 (123, 123, 134) sts. Work rows 1-4 of scalloped shell edging—62 (68, 68,

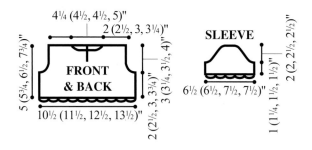

74) sts. Bind off loosely. Sew collar loosely around neck edge. Beg at right back upper neck edge with crochet hook, work 1 row sc down back opening, up left back opening to beg of edging, make buttonloop (ch 5), sc to top of collar. Sew button to right back opposite buttonhole. Sew shoulder seams. Set in sleeves. Sew side and sleeve seams.

Skirt

From fabric, cut 1 (2, 2, 2) skirt pieces each 12 (13, 15, 16)" x 22½ (24½, 26½, 28½)"/30.5 (33, 38, 40.5)cm x 57 (62, 67.5, 72.5) cm. With RS tog and using ⅝"/15mm seam allowance, for smallest size sew back seam for rem sizes sew 2 side seams. Gather one long edge of skirt, adjust gathers to fit; hand-sew to lower edge of bodice, under scalloped edge to beg of eyelet pat. Press ¼"/6mm to WS along rem long edge of skirt, then hem to desired length.

Bring a smile to you little ones face with this knitted doll, designed by Susan Douglas. The bright, contrasting colors are stimulating to a new baby and a simple stockinette-stitch body means quick-to-knit.

KNITTED MEASUREMENTS

12½"/31.5cm tall

MATERIALS

▨ 1 1¾ oz/50g balls (each approx 105 yd/96m) of Cleckheaton *Country 8-ply* by Plymouth Yarn (wool③) each in #1548 blue (A), #1085 yellow (B), #2167 orange (C), #1939 beige (D) and #1102 red (E)

▨ One pair size 6 (4mm) needles or *size to obtain gauge*

▨ One set (4) size 6 (4mm) dpn

▨ Yarn needle

▨ Polyester stuffing

▨ Red colored non-toxic pencil or crayon

GAUGE

22 sts and 30 rows to 4"/10cm over St st using size 6 (4mm) needles.
Take time to check gauge.

Note

Foot, leg, and body are worked on single pointed needles. Arms, head, and ears are worked in rounds on dpn.

RIGHT HALF OF BODY

With single pointed needles and E, cast on 16 sts for foot. Beg with a k row, work in St st for 2 rows. **Inc row (RS)** K, inc 12 sts evenly across—28 sts. Work 9 more rows in St st.

Leg and body

Change to A and k next row on RS, inc 6 sts evenly across—34 sts. Work 29 rows in St st.

Crotch shaping

Next row (RS) Bind off 1 st at beg of next 2 rows. **Next row (RS)** K1, k2tog, k26, ssk, k1—30 sts. Work 29 rows in St st. **Shoulder dec (RS)** K 4, [k2 tog, k2] 3 times, [ssk, k2] 3 times, k2—24 sts. P1 row. Bind off.

LEFT HALF OF BODY

Work as for right half, working leg and body with B instead on A.

NECK RUFFLE

With E, cast on 4 sts. Work in garter st for 108 rows (54 ridges). Bind off.

ARMS

(make 2)

With dpn and D, cast on 12 sts for hand. Divide sts evenly over 3 dpn. Join, placing marker for end of rnd and sl marker every rnd. K 2 rnds. **Next rnd** K, inc 12 sts evenly around—24 sts. K 7 rnds. Change to C. **Next rnd** K, inc 6 sts evenly around—30 sts. K 23 rnds. Bind off.

HEAD

With dpn and C, cast on 36 sts. Divide sts evenly over 3 dpn. Join, placing marker for

end of rnd and sl marker every rnd. K 4 rnds.
Next rnd K, inc 12 sts evenly around—48 sts. K 23 rnds. **Next rnd** [K4, k2tog] 8 times. K 1 rnd. **Next rnd** [K3, k2tog] 8 times. K 1 rnd. **Next rnd** [K2, k2tog] 8 times. K 1 rnd. **Next rnd** [K1, k2tog] 8 times. K 1 rnd. **Next rnd** [K2tog] 8 times—8 sts. Cut yarn, leaving a 12"/30.5cm tail. With yarn needle, thread tail through rem sts and pull tightly together.

EARS

With dpn and D, cast on 12 sts. Divide sts evenly over 3 dpn. Join, placing marker for end of rnd and sl marker every rnd. K 4 rnds. Cut yarn and gather as above.

FINISHING

Sew foot and leg seam to crotch. Gather foot closed. Stuff foot and leg and gather top of foot to define ankle. Sew body pieces together and stuff. Gather bound-off sts slightly to define shoulders. Stuff head. Gather head just below inc rnd to fit into shoulders. Sew head to body. Gather hand closed. Stuff arm and gather top of hand to define wrist. Sew arms to body. Gather the bound-off sts of ears slightly, stuff very lightly and sew to sides of head. Use left-over yarn and straight stitches to embroider eyes, nose and mouth. Knot small pieces of C onto head and trim to 1"/2.5cm. Color cheeks with crayon or pencil.

A clever combination of knit, purl and slip stitches creates the brick wall of this whimsical bunting. Humpty is knit in intarsia. His legs and feet are I-cord, the bow tie and flower petals are all knit separately, creating a 3-dimensional effect. Designed by Nicky Epstein.

SIZES

Instructions are written for size 3 months. Changes for sizes 6 and 9 months are in parentheses.

KNITTED MEASUREMENTS

▒ Chest 22 (25½, 25½)"/56 (64.5, 64.5)cm
▒ Length 21½ (23, 25)"/54.5 (58.5, 63.5)cm
▒ Upper arm 10 (11, 12)"/25.5 (28, 30.5)cm

MATERIALS

▒ 3 (4, 4) 1¾oz/50gr balls (each approx 136yd/125m) of Filatura Di Crosa/Tahki•Stacy Charles, Inc. *501* (wool③) in #102 lt. blue (MC)
▒ 1 (2, 2) balls in #240 rust (A)
▒ 1 ball each in #205 tan (B), #106 white (C), #239 taupe (D), #135 purple (E), #213 olive (F), #136 lt. green (G), #230 blush (H), #176 yellow (I), #238 med blue (small amount) (J)
▒ One pair each sizes 4 and 5 (3.5mm and 3.75mm) needles *or size to obtain gauge*
▒ Size 4 (3.5mm) circular needle, 32"/80cm long
▒ Two size 4 (3.5mm) dpn
▒ Tapestry needle
▒ Five (six, seven) ⅝"/15mm buttons
▒ Stitch markers and holders

GAUGE

22 sts and 29 rows to 4"/10cm over St st using size 5 (3.75mm) needles.
Take time to check gauge.

STITCH GLOSSARY

Brick Pattern
(multiple of 6 sts plus 3)
(**Note**: Slip all sts purlwise)
Row 1 (RS) With B, knit. **Row 2** With B, purl. **Row 3** With A, k4, sl 1; *k5, sl 1; rep from * to last 4 sts, k4. **Row 4** With A, k4, yf, sl 1, yb; *k5, yf, sl 1, yb; rep from * to last 4 sts, k4. **Row 5** With A, p4, yb, sl 1, yf; *p5, yb, sl 1, yf; rep from * to last 4 sts, p4. **Row 6** Rep row 4. **Row 7** With B, knit. **Row 8** With B, purl. **Row 9** With A, k1, sl 1; *k5, sl 1; rep to last st, k1. **Row 10** With A, k1, yf, sl 1, yb; *k5, yf, sl 1, yb; rep from * to last st, k1. **Row 11** With A, p1, yb, sl 1, yf; *p5, yb, sl 1, yf; rep from * to last st, p1. **Row 12** Rep row 10. Rep rows 1-12 for brick pat.

BODY

With larger needles and B, cast on 119 (137, 137) sts. K first and last st of every row for selvage sts (exclude from brick pat count), work in brick pat for 8¾ (10¼, 12¼)"/22 (26, 31)cm, end with a row 2 or 8 of pat. With D, work 6 rows in garter st, dec 2 sts on last row—117 (135, 135) sts.
Note Shaping is *not* shown on chart.
Beg and end as indicated, work in chart pat to end of chart, AT SAME TIME, when piece measures 16½ (17½, 19)"/42 (44.5, 48)cm from beg, end with a WS rows and work as foll:

Divide for fronts and back

Next row (RS) Work 28 (33, 33) sts and place on a holder for right front, work 61 (69, 69) sts for back, place rem 28 (33, 33) sts on a holder for left front. Cont on back sts only to end of chart. **Next row** With MC, work 17 (20, 20) sts and place on a holder for shoulder, work next 27 (29, 29) sts and place on a 2nd holder for back neck, work rem 17 (20, 20) sts and place on a holder for 2nd shoulder.

RIGHT FRONT

Sl sts of right front holder to needle and cont in chart pat until piece measures 20 (21½, 23½)"/50.5 (54.5, 59.5)cm from beg, end with a WS row.

Neck shaping

Next row (RS) Bind off 5 (6, 6) sts (neck edge), work to end. Cont to bind off from neck edge 2 sts 2 (3, 3) times, 1 st 2 (1, 1) times. When same length as back, place rem 17 (20, 20) sts on a holder for shoulder.

LEFT FRONT

Work to correspond to right front, reversing neck shaping. Join shoulders of back and front, using 3-needle-bind-off.

SLEEVES

With smaller needles and MC, cast on 34 (36, 38) sts. K 10 rows. Change to larger needles and cont in St st, inc 1 st each side every other row 9 times, then every 4th row 2 (3, 5) times—56 (60, 66) sts. Work even until piece measures 5½ (6, 7)"/14 (15.5, 18)cm from beg. Bind off.

FINISHING

Block pieces to measurements.

Hood

With RS facing, larger needles and MC, pick up and k 64 (74, 74) sts around neck edge. Work in St st for 5½ (6, 6½)"/14 (15, 16.5)cm, end with a WS row, mark center 2 sts.

Shape hood

Next (dec) row (RS) K to 2 sts before first marker, ssk, k2, k2tog, k to end.

Next row Purl.

Rep last 2 rows 3 times more—56 (66, 66) sts. Divide rem sts and bind off, using 3-needle-bind-off.

Front band

Place markers for 5 (6, 7) buttons along right front for boys or left front for girls, the first one 3"/7.5cm from lower edge, the last one just below neck shaping (hood pick-up) and 3 (4, 5) others spaced evenly between.

With RS facing, size 4 (3.5mm) circular needle and A, beg at right front cast-on edge, pick up and k 42 (48, 58) sts along front opening brick-pat section, change to D and pick up and k 6 sts along the 6 rows of garter st, change to MC and pick up and k 64 sts to beg of neck shaping, 90 sts along entire hood edge, finish straight left front edge to match right—314 (326, 346) sts. Matching colors, work 3 rows garter st.

Next row (RS) Cont in garter st and work buttonholes opposite markers as foll: bind off 3 sts for each buttonhole. On next row, cast on 3 sts over bound-off sts. Work in garter st for 5 more rows. Bind off.

Nose

With larger needles and H make nose-bobble as foll: cast on 1 st, k into front, [back and front] twice of st—5 sts. P 1 row. K 1 row. P 1 row. **Next row** K2tog, k1, k2tog—3 sts. P 1 row. **Next row (RS)** SK2P. Fasten off rem st and sew nose in place as marked on chart.

Legs (make 2)

With dpn and E, cast on 7 sts and work I-cord as foll: ***Next row (RS)** K7, do not turn, slide sts back to beg of needle to work next row from RS; rep from * until I-cord measures 2"/5cm. **Next row** K2tog, k3, k2tog. Cont I-cord over 5 sts for 1¾"/4.5cm, change to I and cont I-cord for 3 rows. **Next row (RS)** (make shoe) Change to D, k and inc 4 sts across row—9 sts. Work in St st for 5 rows. **Next row (RS)** Sl 1, ssk, k3, k2tog, sl 1—7 sts. P 1 row. **Next row** Sl 1, ssk, k1, k2tog, sl 1—5 sts. P 1 row. **Next row** K1, SK2P, k1—3 sts. P 1 row. **Next row** SK2P. Fasten off rem st, leaving end for sewing. With tapestry needle and I, make 3 french knots evenly along center of shoe. Sew beg of legs to beg of main body, and shoes to brick pat.

Bow tie

With larger needles and MC, cast on 9 sts. Work in k1, p1 rib for 2"/5cm. Bind off in rib. Cast on 3 sts and work in rib for ½"/1.5cm. Bind off in rib. Sew small piece around center of larger piece and sew in place as marked on chart.

Flowers (make 7 of each: E and I)

With smaller needles and E (I), cast on 4 sts, *bind off 3 sts, cast on 3 sts; rep from * until there are 6 petals. Fasten off rem st, leaving end for sewing. Loop thread at straight edge of petals and gather. Sew flowers randomly to lower section of brick-pat (see photo). Using opposite colors, make french knot at center flowers. With tapestry needle and F (G), make stems using stem st, and leaves using lazy daisy st (use photo as guide).

With right side of back and fronts tog (buttonhole band overlapping buttonband at center front) sew lower edge seam. Turn to RS and sew lower 2"/5cm of bands closed. Set in sleeves. Sew sleeve seams. Sew on buttons.

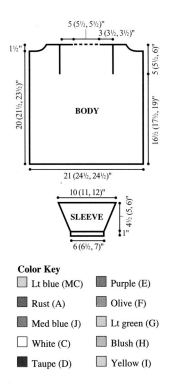

Color Key

- Lt blue (MC)
- Rust (A)
- Med blue (J)
- White (C)
- Taupe (D)
- Purple (E)
- Olive (F)
- Lt green (G)
- Blush (H)
- Yellow (I)

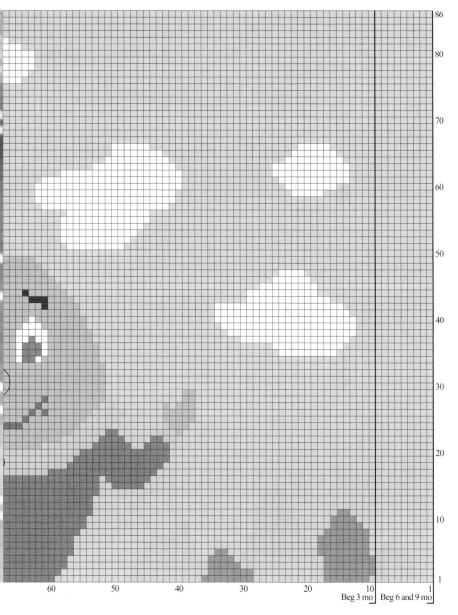

86

80

70

60

50

40

30

20

10

1

60 50 40 30 20 10 1

Beg 3 mo | Beg 6 and 9 mo

Lila Chin designed this trio of cheerful striped bibs. Bordered in reverse stockinette stitch, with a whimsical button for fastening at back of neck, they are the perfect, practical quick-to-knit baby gift.

KNITTED MEASUREMENTS

▓ 8½" x 12"/21.5cm x 30.5cm

MATERIALS

▓ 1 1¾oz/50g balls (each approx 110yd/100m) of Garnstudio/Aurora *Muskat* (cotton③) each in #2 blue (A) and #3 green (B); OR #47 orange (A) and #51 gold (B); OR #34 dk pink (A) and #29 pink (B)

▓ One pair size 3 (3mm) needles *or size to obtain gauge*

▓ Size 3 (3mm) circular needle 40"/100cm long

▓ Stitch holder

▓ One decorative button

GAUGE

28 sts and 38 rows to 4"/10cm over St st using size 3 (3mm) needles.
Take time to check gauge.

STRIPE PATTERN

*4 rows B, 2 rows A; rep from * (6 rows) for stripe pat.

BIB

With B, cast on 52 sts. Work in St st and stripe pat for 7"/17.5cm, end with a WS row.

Neck shaping

Next row (RS) K18 and place sts on a holder for left front, join 2nd ball of yarn and bind off center 16 sts, k to end. Working on right front sts only and cont in stripe pat, work 1 row even.

Next row (RS) K1, ssk, k to end.

Next row (WS) P to last 3 sts, p2tog tbl, p1. Rep last 2 rows until 12 sts rem. Cont in striped pat for 13 rows. Inc 1 st at the beg of every RS row 3 times—15 sts.

Next row (RS) Inc 1 st, k to last 3 sts, k3tog. Work 1 row even.

Rep last 2 rows until 8 sts rem. Bind off.

Sl sts from holder to needle and work left front to correspond right front, reversing shaping as foll: For neck dec, on RS rows, work to last 3 sts, k2tog, k1; on WS rows, p1, p2tog, p to end. Work inc sts at end of RS rows and dec 2 sts at beg of RS rows. Cont as established until 10 sts rem.

Next (buttonhole) row (RS) K3tog, k2, yo, k2tog, k2, inc 1 in last st. Complete as for right front.

FINISHING

With RS facing, circular needle and A, beg at upper left hand tie, pick up and k 284 sts evenly around outside edge of bib. Join and work in rev St st (p every rnd) for 3 rnds. Bind off. Block lightly. Sew on button.

CRIB BLANKET

Muted magic

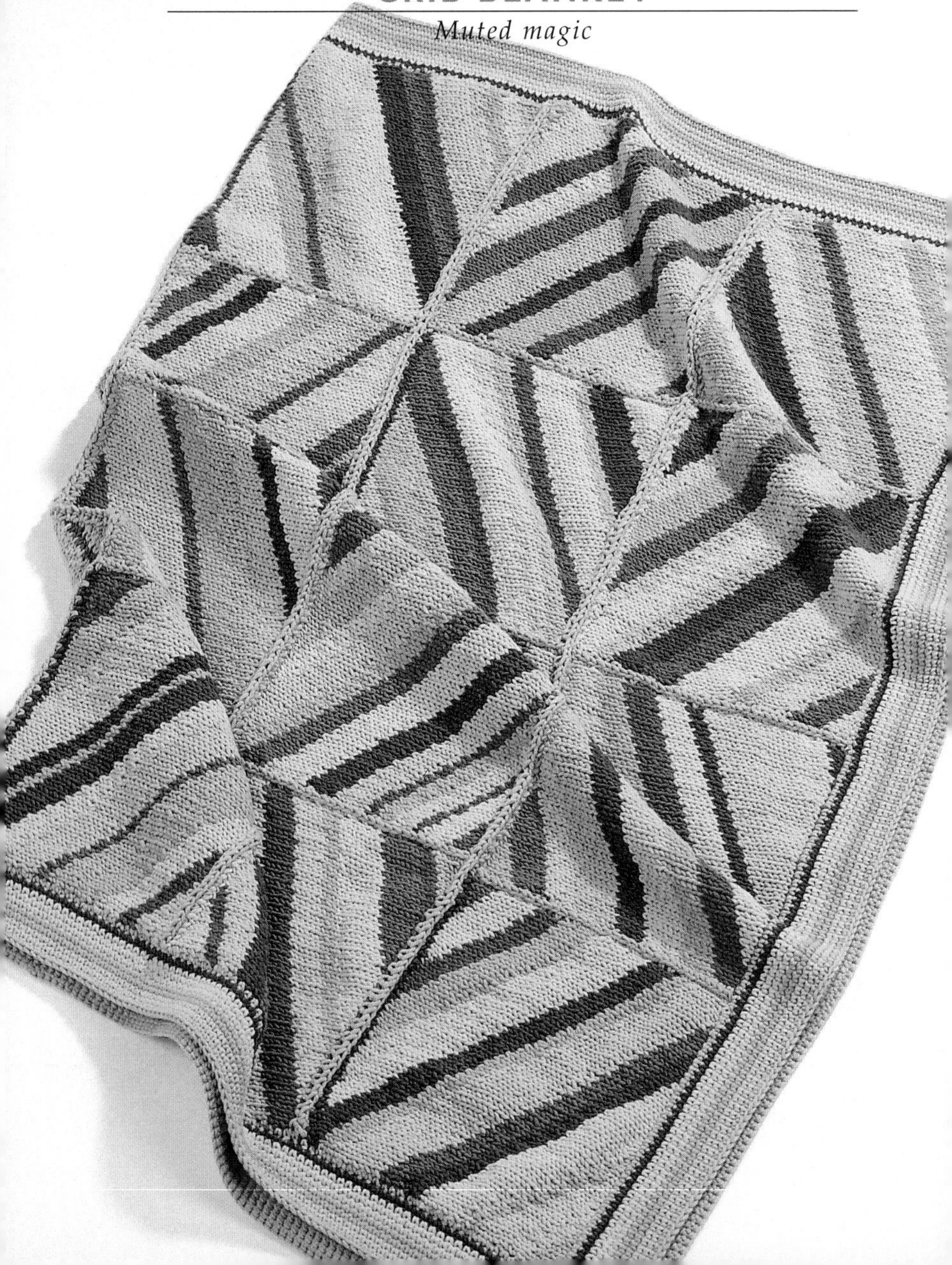

"This blanket is one for doing in front of the TV," says Brandon Mably. He designed this blanket so that the squares are knitted in random diagonal stripes, are joined together by crochet, and then finished with a striped crochet border. This technique can also be used for cushions.

KNITTED MEASUREMENTS
▨ 41" x 56"/104cm x 142cm

MATERIALS
▨ 4 1¾oz/50g balls (each approx 98yd/ 90m of Rowan Yarns *All Seaons Cotton* (cotton/ acrylic ③) each in #199 pale blue (A)
▨ 3 balls each in #194 navy (B), #191 beige (C), #197 lime (D), #198 peach (E), #192 lt green (F), #195 brick, #193 brown (G) and #190 lt grey (H)
▨ One pair size 8 (5mm) needles *or size to obtain gauge*
▨ Size E/4 (3.5mm) crochet hook

GAUGE
18 sts and 22 rows to 4"/10cm over St st using size 8 (5mm) needles.
Take time to check gauge.

SQUARE
(make 24)
Cast on 40 sts. Work in St st for 50 rows in random diagonal stripes (see chart for a sample square). Bind off.

Note To make diagonal stripes, always move color over 1 st *every* row until the color is used up.

FINISHING
With RS facing, crochet hook and A, crochet squares tog with sc, sewing 4 across and 6 down (photo shows blanket folded in half).

Border
With RS facing and crochet hook, work rnds of sc evenly around outside edge of blanket, working 2 sc in corners, in foll stripes: 1 row A, 1 row B, 2 rows C, 1 row D, 2 rows E, 2 rows F, 1 row A.

Sample square

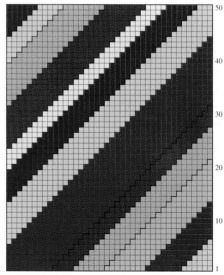

40 sts

Simple chic

Viola Carol designed this jacket using the most basic knit stitch and very simple finishing to create a great project for novice knitters. Crocheted bows accent the pockets and tie the fronts together at the neck.

SIZES

Instructions are written for size 6 months. Changes for sizes 12, 18 and 24 months are in parentheses.

KNITTED MEASUREMENTS

▨ Chest 22 (24, 25, 26)"/56 (61, 63.5, 66)cm
▨ Length 10 (11, 12, 14)"/25.5 (28, 30.5, 35.5)cm
▨ Upper arm 6 (7, 8, 9)"/15 (18, 20.5, 23)cm

MATERIALS

▨ 3 (4, 5, 6) 1¾oz/50g balls (each approx 115yd/106m) of Classic Elite Yarns *Avignon* (cotton/silk④) in #3189 pink (MC)
▨ 1 ball in #3135 green (CC)
▨ One pair size 7 (4.5mm) needles *or size to obtain gauge*
▨ Size G/6 (4.5mm) crochet hook (for ties and bows only)

GAUGE

16 sts and 30 rows to 4"/10cm over garter st using size 7 (4.5mm) needles.
Take time to check gauge.

BACK

With MC, cast on 44 (48, 50, 52) sts.

Work in garter st for 7 (7½, 8, 9½)"/18 (19, 20.5, 24)cm, end with a WS row.

Armhole shaping

Bind off 4 (5, 5, 5) sts at beg of next 2 rows—36 (38, 40, 42) sts. Work even until piece measures 10 (11, 12, 14)"/25.5 (28, 30.5, 35.5)cm from beg, end with a WS row. Bind off all sts.

LEFT FRONT

With MC, cast on 22 (24, 25, 26) sts. Work in garter st for 7 (7½, 8, 9½)"/18 (19, 20.5, 24)cm, end with a WS row.

Armhole shaping

Bind off 4 (5, 5, 5) sts beg at of next RS row—18 (19, 20, 21) sts. Work even until piece measures 8½ (9¼, 10, 12)"/21.5 (23.5, 25.5, 30.5)cm from beg, end with a RS row.

Neck shaping

Next row (WS) Bind off 7 (7, 8, 8) sts (neck edge), work to end. Work even until same length as back. Bind off rem 11 (12, 12, 13) sts for shoulder.

RIGHT FRONT

Work to correspond to left front, reversing all shaping.

SLEEVES

With MC, cast on 24 (28, 32, 36) sts. Work in garter st for 6 (7, 8, 9)"/15 (18, 20.5, 23)cm, end with a WS row.

Cap shaping

Bind off 3 (4, 4, 5) sts at beg of next 2 rows. Work 2 rows even. Dec 1 st at beg of next 10 (12, 14, 16) rows. Bind off 2 (2, 3, 3) sts at beg of next 2 rows. Bind off rem 4 sts.

FINISHING

Block pieces to measurements. Sew shoulder seams. Set in sleeves. Sew side and sleeve seams.

Pockets (make 2)

With MC, cast on 13 (13, 14, 15) sts. Work in garter st for 2 (2½, 3, 3)"/5 (6.5, 7.5, 7.5)cm, end with a WS row. Change to CC and work in St st for 2 rows. Bind off knitwise with CC.

Sew pockets to center fronts, approx 1¼ (1½, 1¾, 2)"/3 (4, 4.5, 5)cm from cast-on edge.

Ties (make 2)

With 2 strands of CC and crochet hook, chain for approx 5 (5½, 6, 6)"/12.5 (14, 15, 15) cm. Tie knot at end. Sew ties to front neck edges.

Bows (make 2)

With 2 strands of CC and crochet hook, chain for approx 10 to 11"/25.5 to 28cm. Tie knots at both ends.

Slip through center of last garter st row on each pocket.

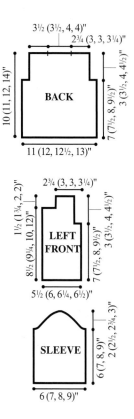

CARRIAGE COVER
Patchwork play

Squares are made separately in a stripe and chevron pattern making this a fine on-the-go project. The squares are sewn together, alternating their directions. An easy cable border is attached later to frame this knitted treasure. Designed by Jo Sharp.

▓ Approx 29" x 39"/74cm x 99cm

▓ 4 1¾oz/50g balls (each approx 107yd/97m) of Jo Sharp/Classic Elite Yarns *8 Ply DK* (wool ③) in #319 violet (A)
▓ 1 ball each in #327 navy (B), #307 wine (C), #316 jade (D), #318 forest (E) and #326 ruby (F)
▓ One pair size 5 (3.75mm) needles o*r size to obtain gauge*
▓ Cable needle
▓ Tapestry needle

31 sts and 39 rows to 5"/12.5cm over chevron pat using size 5 (3.75mm) needles. *Take time to check gauge.*

Chevron Pattern
Rows 1, 3 and 13 (RS) With first color, *p1, k4; rep from *, end p1.
Rows 2 and 12 *K1, p4; rep from *, end k1.
Rows 4 and 8 K2, *p3, k1, p3, k3; rep from *, end k2.

Rows 5 and 9 *P1, k1, p1, [k2, p1] twice, k1; rep from *, end p1.
Rows 6 and 10 *K1, p2, [k1, p1] twice, k1, p2; rep from *, end k1.
Rows 7 and 11 *P1, k3, p3, k3; rep from *, end p1.
Row 14 With 2nd color, purl.
Rows 15 and 26 With 2nd color, rep rows 1-12.
Row 27 With 3rd color, knit.
Rows 28-39 With 3rd color, rep rows 2-13.
Bind off with 3rd color.

Cable Pattern
Row 1 (RS) P3, k10, p3.
Row 2 K1, p1, k1, p10, k1, p1, k1.
Row 3 P3, k1, p1, sl 1 st to cn and hold to *back*, k2, p1 from cn (3-st RPC), sl 2 sts to cn and hold to *front*, p1, k2 from cn (3-st LPC), p1, k1, p3.
Row 4 [K1, p1] twice, k1, p2, k2, p2, [k1, p1] twice, k1.
Row 5 P3, k1, 3-st RPC, p2, 3-st LPC, k1, p3.
Row 6 K1, p1, k1, p3, k4, p3, k1, p1, k1.
Rep rows 1-6 for cable pat.

Cast on 31 sts and work in chevron pat. Make 18 squares using colors E, B and C. Make 17 squares using colors D, A and F.

Block squares. Sew squares tog foll placement diagram.

BORDER STRIPS

With A, cast on 16 sts. Work in cable pat until piece fits along one short edge. Bind off. Work a 2nd strip in same way. Sew strips along 2 short edges. Make 2 more strips to fit along two long edges and sew in place.

Color Key

- ■ Violet (A)
- ■ Navy (B)
- ■ Wine (C)
- ■ Jade (D)
- ■ Forest (E)
- ■ Ruby (F)

Placement diagram

HEIRLOOM BABY BONNET

Pretty baby

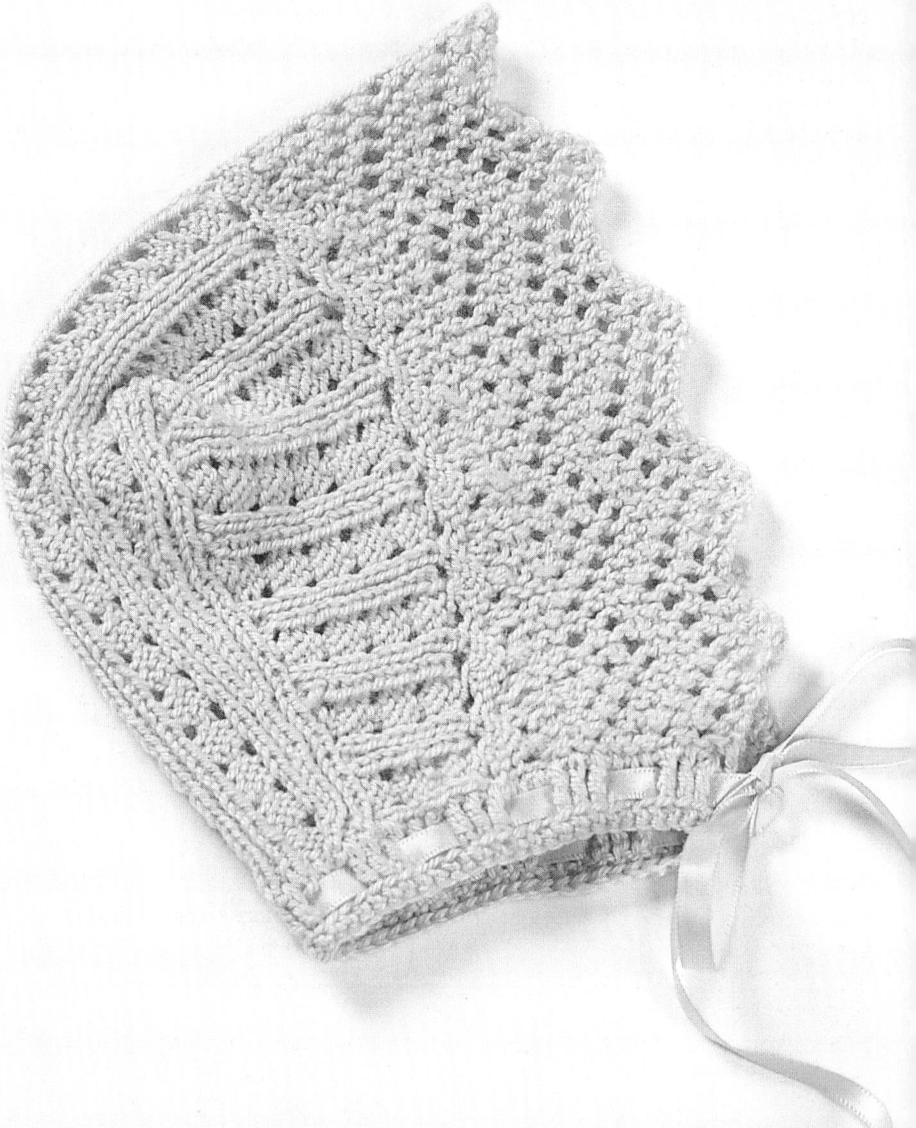

One ball of a luxurious cashmere-and-silk blend fashions a tiny baby bonnet ideal for christening day. The hat's lace band is knit lengthwise and the crown worked by picking up stitches along the side edge of the strip. Designed by Mari Lynn Patrick.

SIZES

Instructions are written for size newborn to 3 months. Changes for sizes 6 to 12 months are in parentheses.

KNITTED MEASUREMENTS

▥ Width around face 12½ (13¾)"/32 (35)cm
▥ Depth of crown 5½ (6½)"/14 (16.5)cm

MATERIALS

▥ 1 .88oz/25g ball (each approx 145yd/132m) of K1C2 *Richesse et Soie* (cashmere/silk①) in #9243 pink
▥ One pair size 2 (2.75mm) needles *or size to obtain gauge*
▥ One size 6 (4mm) needle
▥ Size B/1 (2mm) steel crochet hook

GAUGES

▥ 12-st lace panel is 1¾"/4.5cm wide and 16-row rep is 1¼"/3cm long
▥ 31 sts and 40 rows to 4"/10cm over rib eyelet pat using size 2 (2.75mm) needles.
Take time to check gauges.

STITCH GLOSSARY

Lace Border

Beg at short edge, with size 2 (2.75mm) needles, cast on 12 sts.

Row 1 Sl 1 knitwise, k3, yo, k2tog, *k2, yo, k2tog, yo, k2*.
Row 2 Yo, k2tog, k11.

Row 3 Sl 1, k2, [yo, k2tog] twice; rep between *s of row 1.
Row 4 Yo, k2tog, k12.
Row 5 Sl 1, k3 [yo, k2tog] twice; rep between *s of row 1.
Row 6 Yo, k2tog, k13.
Row 7 Sl 1, k2, [yo, k2tog] 3 times; rep between *s of row 1.
Row 8 Yo, k2tog, k14.
Row 9 Sl 1, k2, k2tog, yo, **k2tog, yo, k2, k2tog, [yo, k2tog] twice, k1 **.
Row 10 Yo, k2tog, k13.
Row 11 Sl 1, k1, k2tog, yo; rep between **s of row 9.
Row 12 Yo, k2tog, k12.
Row 13 Sl 1, k2; rep between**s of row 9.
Row 14 Yo, k2tog, k11.
Row 15 Sl 1, k1; rep between **s of row 9.
Row 16 Yo, k2tog, k10.
Rep rows 1-16 until there are 10 (11) pat reps and lace border measures 12½ (13¾)"/32 (35)cm. Bind off.

BONNET

With RS facing and size 2 (2.75mm) needles, beg along one long edge, pick up and k 97 (109) sts evenly along entire edge.
Row 1 (WS) K1, *p1, yo, k3tog, yo, p1, k1; rep from * to end.
Row 2 P1, k to last st, p1.
Row 3 Knit.
Row 4 (RS) With size 6 (4mm) needles (on this row only), purl.
Row 5 P1, *k5tog tbl, p1; rep from * to end—33 (37) sts.
Row 6 (RS) P1, *yo twice, k1, then [p1 and k1] in horizontal strand between 2 sts, k1; rep from * to end—97 (109) sts.

Beg rib eyelet pat

Row 1 (WS) *K1, p1, k3, p1; rep from *, end k1.

Row 2 P1, *k1, p3, k1, p1; rep from * to end.

Row 3 Rep row 1.

Row 4 P1, *k1, yo, p3tog, yo, k1, p1; rep from * to end. Rep rows 1-4 for rib eyelet pat until piece measures 3½ (4)"/9 (10)cm from one inside lace point, end with pat row 1.

Shape sides

Cont pat, bind off 4 (5) sts at beg of next 14 rows, 5 (4) sts at beg of next 2 rows—31 sts. Work even for 4 (8) rows.

Next row (RS) P2tog, rib to last 2 sts, p2tog.

*Work 5 rows even.

Next (dec) row (RS) Work 3 sts, ssk, rib to last 5 sts, k2tog, work 3 sts.* Rep between *s 5 times more—17 sts. Work

even until piece measures 4½ (5¼)"/11.5 (13.5)cm from last bind off OR until straight side fits along bound-off sides of bonnet. Bind off.

FINISHING

Block piece flat to measurements. Sew side edges of back piece to bound-off edges of bonnet. With crochet hook, working from RS, join in one corner and ch 4, then work 53 (59) tr in each st along lower edge. Ch 1, turn, 1 sc in back lp of each tr. Fasten off.

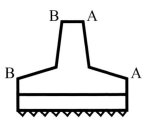

BUILDING BLOCKS
Knock 'em down

For Intermediate Knitters

This trio of knitted cubes is perfect for baby's playroom. Three light, firm blocks can be stacked up, knocked over, tossed around, and sat on for hours. All designed by Jean Moss.

SIZES
- Small block 4½"/11.5cm square
- Medium block 7½"/19cm square
- Large block 10"/25.5cm square

MATERIALS
- 3½oz/100g balls (each approx 151yd/140m) of Rowan Yarns *Magpie Aran* (wool ④)
- 1 ball each in #684 berry, #301 pumice, #002 natural, #313 tinkerbell, #314 laurel, #318 misty #771 porridge, #450 dapple, #770 dolphin
- 3½oz/100g balls (each approx 184yd/170m) of Rowan Yarns *Magpie Tweed* (wool ④)
- 1 ball each in #768 pesto, #766 sienna, #775 jewel, #778 harbour
- 1¾oz/50g balls (each approx 184yd/170m) of Rowan Yarns *True 4 Ply Botany* (wool ②) (**note** hold two strands tog)
- 1 ball each in #572 tuscan, #571 lavender, #564 blond
- One pair size 7 (4.5mm) needles *or size to obtain gauge*
- Foam squares cut to fit

GAUGE
18 sts and 24 rows to 4"/10cm over St st using size 7 (4.5mm) needles.
Take time to check gauge.

Notes
1 Always sl the first st of every row and k into the back of the last st of every row. The resulting notches can be matched when sewing.

2 When working with *True 4 Ply Botany*, use two strands held tog.

SMALL BLOCK
With background color, cast on 23 sts and work 29 rows of each chart. Bind off with background color.

FINISHING
Sew 6 squares tog to form a cube, leaving one seam open. Stuff block and sew rem siea, using a small invisibl slip st.

MEDIUM BLOCK
With background color, cast on 35 sts and work 45 rows of each chart. Finish as for small block.

LARGE BLOCK
With background color, cast on 45 sts and work 61 rows of each chart. Finish as for small block.

Color Key
- Pesto
- Blonde
- Dapple
- Pumice
- Harbour
- Berry
- Misty
- Jewel
- Natural
- Tinkerbell
- Sienna
- Laurel
- Porridge
- Lavender
- Dolphin
- Tuscan

Small Block

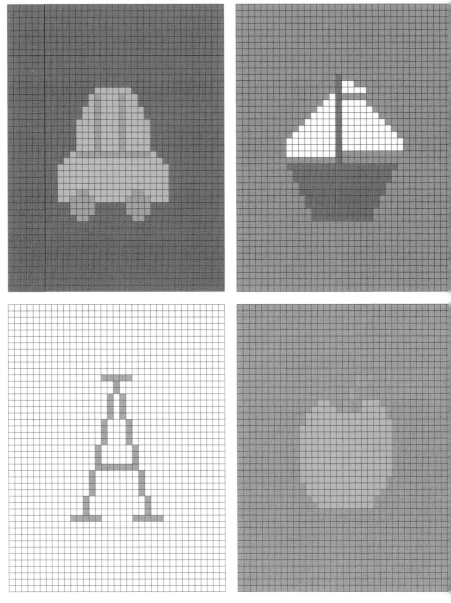

Medium Block

Large Block

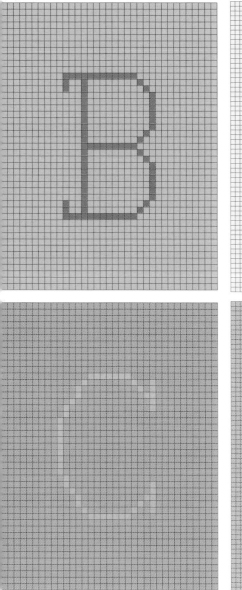

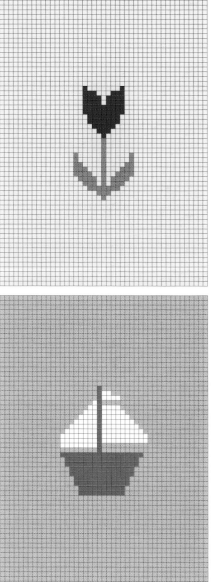

Knit all in one piece, with minimal finishing, this project is easy enough for a new knitter to tackle. The playful beach ball buttons add a bit of whimsy. Designed by Loren Cherensky.

SIZES

Instructions are written for size 6 months. Changes for sizes 12, 18 and 24 months are in parentheses.

KNITTED MEASUREMENTS

▪ Chest 21 (23, 25, 26)"/53.5 (58.5, 63.5, 66)cm
▪ Length 10 (11, 12, 14)"/25.5 (28, 30.5, 35.5)cm
▪ Upper arm 9 (9½, 10, 11)"/23 (24, 25.5, 28.5)cm

MATERIALS

▪ 2 (3, 3, 4) 2½oz/70g balls (each approx 168yd/154m) of Lion Brand Yarn Co. *Micro Spun* (acrylic④) in #113 red
▪ One pair size 7 (4.5mm) needles *or size to obtain gauge*
▪ 4 (4, 5, 5) ⅝"/15mm buttons by JHB International
▪ Stitch markers

GAUGE

20 sts and 28 rows to 4"/10cm over St st using size 7 (4.5mm) needles.
Take time to check gauge.

Note

Sweater is worked in one piece.

BACK

Cast on 53 (57, 63, 65) sts. Work in garter st for 9 (9, 11, 11) rows. Cont in St st (beg with a k row on RS) until piece measures 5½ (6¼, 7, 8½)"/14 (16, 18, 21.5)cm from beg, end with a WS row.

SLEEVES

Cast on 5 (6, 7, 10) sts at beg of next 10 rows, then 6 (4, 3, 5) sts at beg of next 2 rows—115 (125, 139, 175) sts.

Next row Work 7 (7, 8, 8) sts in garter st, work St st to last 7 (7, 8, 8) sts, work garter st to end. Cont as established until piece measures 10 (11, 12, 14)"/25.5 (28, 30.5, 35.5)cm from beg, end with a WS row, place marker each at end of needle (center sleeve cuff).

Neck shaping, divide fronts

Next row (RS) Work 47 (52, 58, 76) sts, join 2nd ball of yarn and bind off center 21 (21, 23, 23) sts, work to end. Working both sides at once, work even for 1½ (1½, 1¾, 1¾)"/4 (4, 4.5, 4.5)cm, end with a WS row. Cast on 13 (13, 14, 14) sts at each neck edge—60 (65, 72, 90) sts for each front. Work even for 5 rows, working 5 (5, 6, 6) sts at each front edge in garter st for button/buttonhole bands.

Next row (RS) Cont in pat, work first buttonhole (make buttonhole on right front for girls as foll: Work to garter-st band, k1 (1, 2, 2), yo, k2tog tbl, k2. Make buttonhole on left front for boys as foll: K2, k2tog, yo, k1 (1, 2, 2). Cont to make 3 (3, 4, 4) more buttonholes every 2 (2½, 2, 2½)"/5 (6.5, 5, 6.5)cm, AT SAME TIME, when piece measures 2¾ (3, 3¼, 3¾)"/7 (7.5, 8.5, 9.5)cm from markers, shape sleeves as foll: Bind off 6 (4, 3, 5) sts from each sleeve edge once, then 5 (6, 7, 10) sts 5 times—29 (31, 34, 35) sts. Work even, cont buttonholes as before, until fronts measure same as back to beg of bottom garter st edge, end with a WS row. P 9 (9, 11, 11) rows. Bind off knitwise on WS.

FINISHING

Block piece to measurements. Sew side and sleeve seams. Sew on buttons opposite buttonholes.

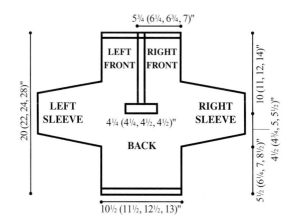

For Intermediate Knitters

Gitta Schrade designed these cute overalls in a durable cotton yarn to stand up to even the most active child. Buttons on the inside of the legs make for easy changing, and the varying width of the stripe pattern adds a touch of fun.

SIZES
Instructions are written for size 6 months. Changes for sizes 12, 18 and 24 months are in parentheses.

KNITTED MEASUREMENTS
▢ Chest 20 (23, 24, 26)"/51 (58.5, 61, 66)cm
▢ Length 19 (24, 27, 30)"/48 (61, 68.5, 76)cm (with ribbed cuff folded up 1½"/ 4cm)

MATERIALS
▢ 2 (3, 3, 3) 1¾oz/50g balls (each approx 123yd/110m) of Reynolds/JCA *Saucy Sport* (cotton③) each in #117 deep ocean (A), #869 chambray (B)
▢ Sizes 3 and 5 (3mm and 3.75mm) circular needle 16"/40 cm long *or size to obtain gauge*
▢ One set (4) size 3 (3mm) dpn
▢ Ten (ten, twelve, twelve) ½"/13mm buttons
▢ Stitch markers and holders

GAUGE
22 sts and 32 rows to 4"/10cm over St st using size 5 (3.75mm) needles.
Take time to check gauge.

STITCH GLOSSARY
Small Stripe Pattern
*2 rows B, 2 rows A; rep from * (4 rows) for small stripe pat.
Large Stripe Pattern
*4 rows A, 4 rows B; rep from * (8 rows) for large stripe pat.

OVERALLS
Right Leg
With dpn and A, cast on 48 (48, 52, 52) sts. Divide sts evenly over 3 needles. Join, taking care not to twist sts on needle. Place marker for end of rnd and sl marker every rnd. Work in k2, p2 rib for 4"/10cm, bind off 2 sts at end of last rnd—46 (46, 50, 50) sts.
Beg stripe pats
Change to circular needle (used back and forth) and cont in St st as foll:
Join B and work in small stripe pat, AT SAME TIME, inc 1 st each side every 4th row 4 (8, 7, 10) times—54 (62, 64, 70) sts. Work even until piece measures 4 (5½, 7½, 8)"/10 (14, 19, 20.5)cm above rib, end with a WS row. Place sts on holder.
Left Leg
Work as for right leg; do *not* place on holder.
Leg joining
Next rnd (RS) With circular needle, cont in small stripe pat, cast on 1 st at beg of left leg, k across sts of left leg, cast on 2 sts, k across the sts from right leg holder, cast on 1 st, join to work in rnds and place marker for beg of rnd (and center back)— 112 (128, 132, 144) sts.

BODY

Cont in small stripe pat for approx 1¾ (2¼, 2¾, 3)"/4.5 (6, 7, 7.5)cm, end with 2 rnds of B.

Cont in large stripe pat until body measures 6½ (9¾, 10½, 12½)"/16.5 (24.5, 26.5, 31.5)cm above leg joining, end with 4 rows of A. Using B only, work for 1½"/4cm.

Armhole shaping

Next rnd K 19 (22, 23, 25) sts, bind off 18 (20, 20, 22) sts, k until there are 38 (44, 46, 50) sts on RH needle, join 2nd ball of yarn and bind off 18 (20, 20, 22) sts. Place the 38 (44, 46, 50) front sts on holder.

BACK

Work even in St st over 38 (44, 46, 50) sts of back for 3½ (3¾, 4, 4½)"/9 (9.5, 10, 11.5)cm, end with a WS row.

Neck shaping

Next row (RS) K 6 (8, 9, 10) sts for right shoulder, join 2nd ball of yarn and bind off center 26 (28, 28, 30) sts, k rem 6 (8, 9, 10) sts for left shoulder. Working both sides at once, cont even for 1"/2.5cm, end with a WS row. Bind off.

FRONT

Work as for back until armhole measures 2¼ (2¼, 2¼, 2¾)"/5.5 (5.5, 5.5, 7)cm, end with a WS row.

Neck shaping

Next row (RS) K 6 (8, 9, 10) sts for left shoulder, join 2nd ball of yarn and bind off center 26 (28, 28, 30) sts, k rem 6 (8,

9, 10) sts for right shoulder. Working both sides at once, cont even for 3 (3¼, 3½, 3½)"/7.5 (8, 9, 9)cm, end with a WS row.

Next (buttonhole) row (RS) K1, yo, k2tog, k 0 (2, 3, 4), ssk, yo, k1. P 1 row. Place sts on holder.

FINISHING

Left armhole edging

With RS facing and smaller circular needle (used back and forth), beg at back left shoulder edge, pick up and k 82 (88, 92, 100) sts along armhole edge, end at top of front left shoulder edge. Mark the st closest to each armhole corner. **Next row (WS)** Work in k1, p1 rib. **Next row (RS)** *Rib to 1 st before marked st, sl 2, k1, psso; rep from * once more; rib to last st, M1, k1. Rep last 2 rows once more—76 (82, 86, 94) sts. Bind off in rib on WS.

Right armhole edging

Work to correspond to left armhole edging.

Front neck edging

With RS facing and smaller circular needle (used back and forth), pick up and k the 6 (8, 9, 10) sts from holder for left shoulder, pick up and k 72 (76, 78, 80) sts along front neck, k the 6 (8, 9, 10) sts from holder for right shoulder, mark the corner st at each shoulder and the front neck corner sts—84 (92, 96, 100) sts. **Next row (WS)** Work in k1, p1 rib. **Next row (RS)** Work into back and front of first st, rib to first marker, M1, k1, M1; *rib to 1 st before next marker, sl 2, k1, psso; rep from * once more; rib to last marker, M1, k1, M1, rib to last st, work into back and front of last st. Rep last 2 rows once more—88 (96, 100, 104) sts. Bind off in rib on WS.

Back neck edging

With RS facing and smaller circular needle (used back and forth), pick up and k 47 (49, 49, 51) sts along back neck (not including bound-off shoulder edge), mark the corner st at each shoulder and the front neck corner sts. **Next row (WS)** Work in k1, p1 rib. **Next row (RS)** *Rib to 1 st before first marker, sl 2, k1, psso; rep from * once more; rib to end. Rep last 2 rows once more—39 (41, 41, 43) sts. Bind off in rib on WS.

Sew rib tog at mitered edges on front shoulders.

Buttonband

With RS facing and smaller circular needle (used back and forth) pick up k 53 (73, 99, 105) sts along back leg opening. Work in k1, p1 rib for 3 rows. Bind off in rib. Place markers for 6 (6, 8, 8) buttons—3 (3, 4, 4) buttons up each leg, with the first and last one ¾"/2cm from lower edge and center crotch and rem spaced evenly between.

Buttonhole band

With RS facing, pick up sts along front leg opening and work as for buttonband. Make buttonholes in first rib row (on WS) opposite markers as foll: k2tog, yo. Sew sides of rib bands in place.

Sew on buttons.

Fold leg ribbed cuffs up 1½"/4cm.

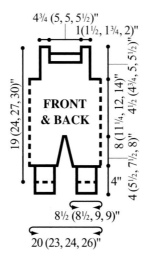

BABY BOOTIES
First steps

Very Easy Very Vogue

Quick and easy-to-knit, these colorful booties are a perfect shower gift. The ribbon ties are woven through the eyelet row to secure shoes on pint-sized feet! Designed by Jean Guirguis.

SIZE

Instructions are written for size 6 months. Changes for size 12 months are in parentheses.

KNITTED MEASUREMENTS

▓ Sole measures 4 (5)"/10 (12.5)cm

MATERIALS

▓ 1 1¾oz /50g balls (each approx 117yd/108m) of Sesia/Lane Borgosesia *Windsurf* (cotton②) each in #109 lime (A), #479 turquoise (B) and #51 white (C)

▓ One pair size 4 (3.5mm) needles *or size to obtain gauge*

▓ ½ yd/.5m white satin ribbon, ⅛"/3mm wide

GAUGE

24 sts and 32 rows to 4"/10cm over St st using size 4 (3.5mm) needles.
Take time to check gauge.

BOOTIE

Beg at sole center, with A cast on 37 (41) sts.

Row 1 (WS) K18 (20), mark center st, k to end.

Row 2 K1, yo, k to marked st, yo, k1, yo, k to last st, yo, k1—41 (45) sts. **Next row** Knit, working yo's tbl. Rep last 2 rows 3 times more—53 (57) sts. Change to B: K 1 row on RS. Beg with a WS row, work in k1, p1 rib for 9 (11) rows.

Next row (RS) Rib 22 (24) sts B, k8 C (for instep), SKP, turn.

*Next row With C, sl 1, purlwise, p7, p2tog, turn.

Next row Sl 1 knitwise, k7, SKP, turn. Rep from * 5 times more.

Next row (WS) Sl 1 purlwise, p7, p2tog, turn. Cut C. Join B at beg of next (RS) row. There are 39 (43) sts.

Next row (RS) K14 (16), k2tog, k7, SKP, k14 (16). With B, work 3 rows in St st, then k 2 rows.

Next (eyelet) row (RS) K1, *k2tog, yo; rep from *, end k2. With B, k 3 rows.

Next row (RS) *K1B, k1C; rep from * to end. With C, work 2 rows St st. **Next row (RS)** *K1B, k1C; rep from * to end. With A, k 6 rows. Bind off.

FINISHING

Block booties lightly. Placing cast-on edge tog, sew sole seam, then sew back seam. Weave ribbon through eyelet row and tie at center front.

ARAN BABY BUNTING

Bundle of joy

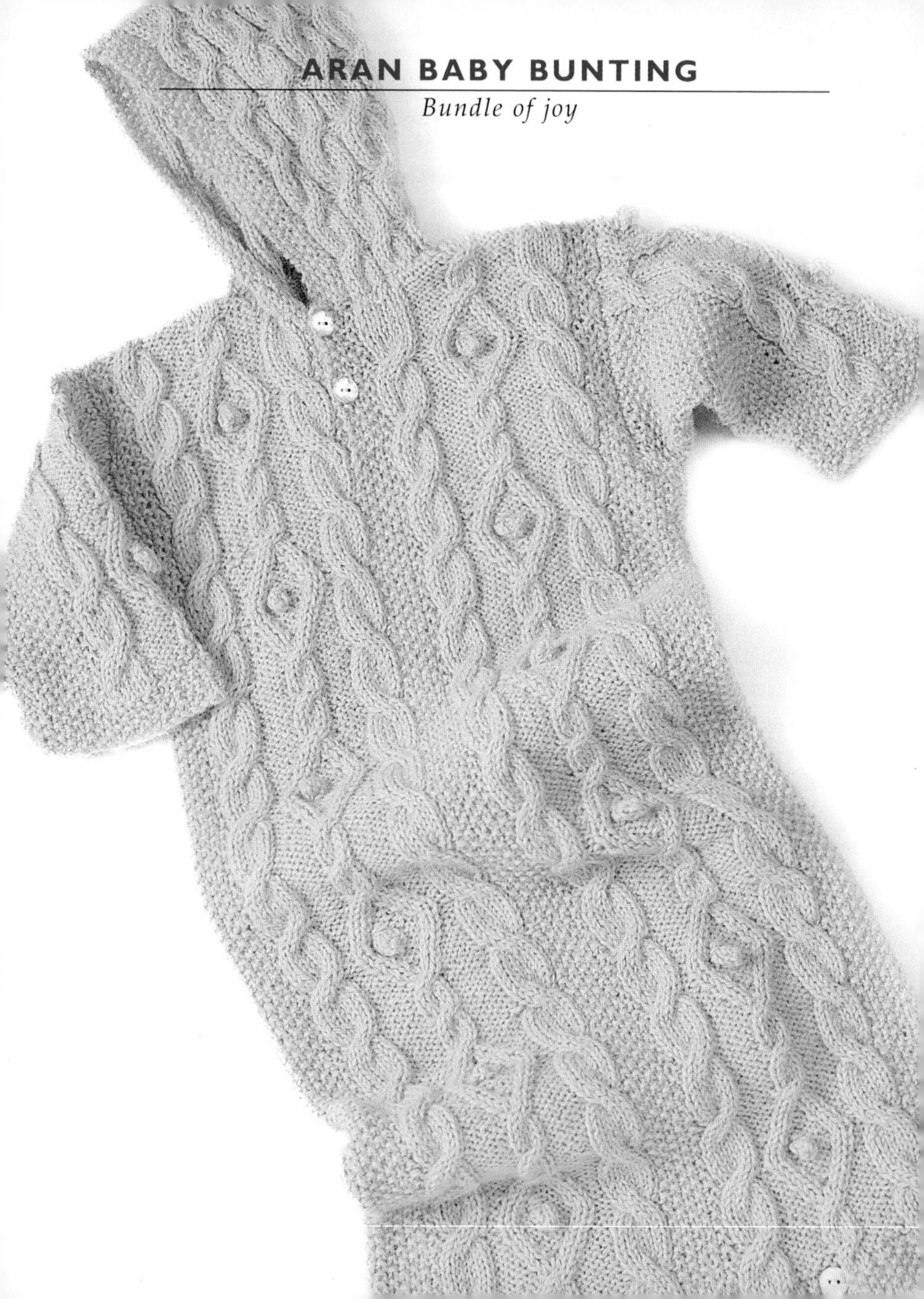

For Experienced Knitters

A rich combination of cables, seed stitch, and soft, luxurious cashmere yarn creates an elegant bunting fit for a little royal. A button closure at the lower edge makes changing diapers a breeze, and the extra length in the body keeps wriggling feet toasty warm. Designed by Kirsten Cowan.

SIZES
Instructions are written for size 3 months. Changes for sizes 6 and 9 months are in parentheses.

KNITTED MEASUREMENTS
■ Chest 20 (22, 25)"/51 (56, 63.5)cm
■ Length 21½ (23, 25)"/54.5 (58.5, 63.5)cm
■ Upper arm 9 (10, 11)"/23 (25.5, 28)cm

MATERIALS
■ 6 1¾oz/50g balls (each approx 144yd/133m) of Filanda/Trendsetter Yarns *Alpaca* (alpaca③) in #48 lavender
■ One pair size 4 (3.5mm) needles, *or size to obtain gauge*
■ Size E/4 (3.5mm) crochet hook for optional car seat buckle slit
■ Cable needle
■ Seven ½"/13mm buttons
■ Stitch markers

GAUGE
24 sts and 34 rows to 4"/10cm over St st using size 4 (3.5mm) needles.
Take time to check gauge.

STITCH GLOSSARY
Seed Stitch
Row 1 *K1, p1; rep from * to end.
Row 2 K the purl and p the knit sts.
Rep row 2 for seed st.

6-st LC (RC) Sl 3 sts to cn and hold to *front (back)*, k3, k3 from cn.
4-st RC
Sl 2 sts to cn and hold to *back*, k2, k2 from cn.
2/1 LPC
Sl 2 st to cn and hold to *front*, p1, k2 from cn.
1/2 RPC
Sl 1 st to cn and hold to *back*, k2, p1 from cn.
MB (Make Bobble)
K1, p1, k1, p1 into next st, turn, p4, turn, k4, turn, p4, turn, [k2tog] twice, then with point of LH needle, sl first st over 2nd st.

Panel Pattern (over 16 sts)
Rows 1, 5, 7 (RS) P6, k4, p6.
Row 2 and all WS rows K the knit sts and p the purl sts.
Rows 3 and 9 P6, 4-st RC, p6.
Row 11 P5, 1/2 RPC, 2/1 LPC, p5.
Row 13 P4, 1/2 RPC, p2, 2/1 LPC, p4.
Row 15 P3, 1/2 RPC, p4, 2/1 LPC, p3.
Row 17 P2, 1/2 RPC, p3, MB, p2, 2/1 LPC, p2.
Row 19 P2, 2/1 LPC, p6, 1/2 RPC, p2.
Row 21 P3, 2/1 LPC, p4, 1/2 RPC, p3.
Row 23 P4, 2/1 LPC, p2, 1/2 RPC, p4.
Row 25 P5, 2/1 LPC, 1/2 RPC, p5.
Row 27 Rep row 3.
Row 29 Rep row 1.
Row 30 Rep row 2.

6-st LC (RC) Cable
Rows 1, 3 and 5 K6.
Row 2 and all WS rows P6.
Row 7 6-st LC (RC).
Row 9 K6.
Row 10 P6.
Directions for optional slit for car seat buckle
Work until Back (Front) measures 9½ (10½, 11½)"/24 (26.5, 29) cm from beg.
Next row Work 26 (30, 35) sts, bind off 21 sts, work to end.
Next row Work 26 (30, 35) sts, turn, cast on 21 sts, turn, work to end.

BACK
Cast on 65 (71, 81) sts. Work in seed st for 7 rows. P next row on WS and inc 8 (10, 10) sts across—73 (81, 91) sts.
Beg pats
Next row (RS) Work 4 (8, 12) sts in seed st, *p1, row 1 of 6-st LC cable, work row 1 of 16-st panel pat, row 1 of 6-st RC cable, p1*; work 5 (5, 7) sts; rep from * to * once more, work 4 (8, 12) sts.
Row 2 and all WS rows Work 4 (8, 12) sts in seed st, *k1, p6 (row 2 of RC cable), work row 2 of 16-st panel pat, p6 (row 2 of LC cable), k1*; work 5 (5, 7) sts seed st; rep from * to * once more; work 4 (8, 12) sts seed st. Cont in pats as established, working 30 rows of 16-st Panel pat and 10 rows each of 6-st LC (RC) throughout. (Work optional slit if required). Work until piece measures 17 (18, 19½)"/43 (46, 49.5) cm from beg, end with a WS row.

Armhole shaping
Bind off 4 (4, 6) sts beg next 2 rows—65 (73, 79) sts. Work even until armhole measures 4½ (5, 5½)"/11.5 (12.5, 14) cm. Bind off.

FRONT
Cast on 65 (71, 81) sts. Work in seed st for 4 rows.
Next (buttonhole) row (RS) Work 6 (7, 8) sts in seed st, *k2tog, yo, work 11 (12, 14) sts seed st; rep from * 3 times more, k2tog, yo, 5 (6, 7) sts seed st. Work in seed st for 2 more rows. P 1 row and inc 8 (10, 10) sts across—73 (81, 91) sts.
Work as for back until armhole measures 1 (1, 1½)"/2.5 (2.5, 4) cm, end with a WS row.
Placket opening
Next row (RS) Work 35 (39, 43) sts, with 2nd ball of yarn cast on 5 (5, 7) sts, work to end. Working both sides at once, work the extra cast-on sts in seed st, work even for 2 (2½, 2½)"/5 (6.5, 6.5)cm ending with a WS row, AT SAME TIME work buttonholes at center seed st band of left front for boys and right front for girls, the first one ¾ (1, 1)"/2 (2.5, 2.5)cm from beg of placket opening, and the 2nd 1"/2.5cm above the first one, as foll: (RS) *For boys* Work to last 5 (5, 7) sts, work 2 (2, 3) sts seed st, yo, k2tog, work to end. *For Girls* work 1 (1, 2) sts seed st, k2tog, yo, work to end.
Neck shaping
Place the 5 (5, 7) placket sts of each front on holder. Bind off 3 sts each neck edge

once, then dec 1 st next 6 (7, 7) rows. Work even until same length as back to shoulder. Bind off rem 21 (24, 26) sts each side for shoulders.

SLEEVES

Cast on 37 (41, 43) sts. Work in seed st for 7 rows. P next row on WS and inc 5 sts across—42 (46, 48) sts.

Beg pats

Next row (RS) Work 6 (8, 9) sts in seed st, p1, row 1 of 6-st LC cable, work row 1 of 16-st panel pat, row 1 of 6-st RC cable, p1, seed st 6 (8, 9) sts.

Cont in pats as established, AT SAME TIME, inc 1 st each side on next row then every 4th row 7 (8, 10) times more (working inc sts into seed st)—58 (64, 70) sts. Work even until piece measures 6 (7, 8)"/15 (18, 20.5)cm from beg. Bind off.

FINISHING

Block pieces to measurements.

Sew lower edge of button placket in place behind buttonhole placket.

(Optional car seat buckle: Sc around openings.)

Sew shoulder seams.

HOOD

With RS facing, seed st across the 5 (5, 7) sts of right front placket, pick up and k 13 (15, 15) sts along right front neck edge, pick up and k 23 (25, 27) sts along back neck, 13 (15, 15) sts down left front neck edge, seed st the 5 (5, 7) sts of left front placket—59 (65, 71) sts.

Next Row (WS) Seed st 5 (5, 7) sts, p to last 5 (5, 7) sts, AT SAME TIME, inc 25 (27, 33) sts evenly across, end with seed st 5 (5, 7)—84 (92, 104) sts.

Beg pat

Next row (RS) Seed st 5 (5, 7) sts; *p2, row 1 of 6-st RC cable; rep from * to last 7 (7, 9) sts, p2, seed st 5 (5, 7) sts.

Work in pat as established, work the 10 rows of cable pat 6 (6, 7) times in total, then work rows 1 and 2 once more.

Slip half the sts to spare needle and bind off using 3-needle-bind-off .

Set in sleeves, sewing last ¾ (¾, 1)"/2 (2, 2.5)cm at top of sleeve to bound-off armhole sts. Sew side and sleeve seams.

Sew on buttons.

3 (3½, 4)"

3 (3¼, 3½)"

4½ (5, 5½)"

21½ (23, 25)"

FRONT & BACK

17 (18, 19½)"

10 (11, 12½)"

9 (10, 11)"

SLEEVE

5 (6, 7)"

1"

6 (6½, 7)"

These whimsical charmers, designed by Kristin Nicholas, are knit up quickly in basic stockinette-stitch tubes in bright colors to catch an infant's eye. Insert a small bell to make a rattle. French knots create the face and polka dots and tied fringe become the hair.

KNITTED MEASUREMENTS
▓ Approx 10"/25.5cm tall

MATERIALS
▓ 1¾oz/50g balls (each approx 95yd/85m) of Classic Elite Yarns *Tapestry* (wool/mohair ③) in small amounts of assorted colors
▓ One set (4) size 5 (3.75mm) dpn *or size to obtain gauge*
▓ Tapestry needle
▓ Small ball with bell (or cat toy)

GAUGE
22 sts and 26 rows to 4"/10cm over St st using size 5 (3.75mm) needles.
Take time to check gauge.

LEGS
(Make 2)
Using desired color, cast on 13 sts. Divide sts over 3 needles and join, taking care not to twist sts on needles. Work in St st (k every rnd) for 3½"/9cm or to desired length.
Next rnd *K2tog; rep from *, end k1—7 sts. Cut yarn and pull through rem sts to tighten.

ARMS
(Make 2)
Cast on 11 sts using desired color. Divide sts over 3 needles and join, taking care not to twist sts on needles. Work in St st for 3"/7.5cm or to desired length.
Next rnd *K2tog; rep from *, end k1—6 sts. Cut yarn and pull through rem sts to tighten.

BODY
Cast on 13 sts using desired color. Divide sts over 3 needles and join, taking care not to twist sts on needles. K 1 rnd.
Next rnd K in front and back of each st around—26 sts. Work even until piece measures 3½"/9cm from beg.
Next rnd *K2tog; rep from * around—13 sts.
Next rnd *K2tog, k2; rep from *, end k1—10 sts.
Next rnd *K1, k2tog; rep from *, end k1—7 sts.
K 2 rnds for neck.

HEAD
Change color and k 1 rnd.
Next rnd K in front and back of each st around—14 sts.
Next rnd *K1, k in front and back of next st; rep from * around—21 sts. K 6 rnds.
Next rnd *K1, k2tog; rep from * around—14 sts.
Next rnd *K2tog; rep from * around—7 sts. Cut yarn and pull through rem sts to tighten.

FINISHING

Stuff head with odd bits of yarn or stuffing.

Hint

Using a similar color yarn or old sock which will not show through the knit sts when stuffed firmly.

Wrap bell or cat toy in yarn and place into body cavity. Cont stuffing around rattle. Sew bottom opening of body. Stuff legs and arms. Sew openings shut. Attach arms and legs at sides.

HAIR

Using double strand of yarn, work fringed hair. With tapestry needle threaded with double yarn, leave a long tail, take a small st to anchor hair, leave loop for hair and take another small st to anchor second length of hair. Work in various colors and trim to desired length.

Work french knots for eyes and nose. Work assorted colors of french knots over body to decorate. Work small running st around neck and tie in a bow if desired.

Very Easy Very Vogue

Every baby deserves a little luxury. Silk ribbon embroidery graces the fronts and collar of this simple seed stitch cardigan, knit with sumptuous cashmere. Designed by Jean Guirguis.

SIZES

Instructions are written for size 6 months. Changes for sizes 12, 18 and 24 months are in parentheses.

KNITTED MEASUREMENTS
■ Chest 21½ (23½, 25¼, 27)"/54.5 (59.5, 64, 68.5)cm
■ Length 10½ (11, 12, 14)"/26.5 (28, 30.5, 35.5)cm
■ Upper arm 9 (9½, 10½, 11½)"/23 (24, 26.5, 28.5)cm

MATERIALS
■ 4 (5, 5, 6) .88oz/25g balls (each approx 120yd/110m) of Grignasco/JCA *Cashmere* (cashmere②) in #406 powder blue
■ One pair size 2 (2.5mm) needles *or size to obtain gauge*
■ 5 (5, 6, 7) ⅜"/10mm buttons
■ Mokuba silk ribbon in: 4mm wide: Lt. Blue, Dk. Blue, Lt. Pink, Med. Pink, Dk. Pink, Yellow, Dk Green
7mm wide: Lt. Green
■ Sewing thread in light, medium and dark pink
■ Tapestry and sewing needle
■ Stitch markers
■ Stitch holders

GAUGE
28 sts and 50 rows to 4"/10cm over seed st using size 2 (2.5mm) needles.
Take time to check gauge.

STITCH GLOSSARY
Seed stitch
Row 1 (RS) K1, *p1, k1; rep from * to end.
Row 2 P the knit sts and k the purl sts.
Rep row 2 for seed st.

BACK
Cast on 77 (83, 89, 95) sts. Work in seed st until piece measures 10½ (11, 12, 14)"/26.5 (28, 30.5, 35.5)cm, end with a WS row.
Place 23 (25, 28, 30) sts on a holder for right shoulder, center 31 (33, 33, 35) sts on a 2nd holder for back neck and rem 23 (25, 28, 30) sts on a 3rd holder for left shoulder.

LEFT FRONT
Cast on 35 (39, 41, 45) sts. Work in seed st until piece measures 8½ (9, 10, 12)"/21.5 (23, 25.5, 30.5)cm from beg, end with a RS row.
Neck shaping
Next row (WS) Bind off 6 sts (neck edge), work to end. Cont to bind off from neck edge 2 sts once, then dec 1 st every other row 4 (6, 5, 7) times. Work even until same length as back. Place rem 23 (25, 28, 30) sts on holder for shoulder.

RIGHT FRONT

Work to correspond to left front, reversing shaping.

FINISHING

Block pieces to measurements.
Join fronts to back at shoulders, using three needle bind-off.
Place markers 4 (4¾, 5, 5¾)"/10 (11.5, 13, 14) cm down from shoulder at back and front.

SLEEVES

With RS facing, pick up and k 63 (67, 73, 79) sts along front and back between markers. Work in seed st for 1"/2.5cm.

Dec 1 st each side on next row, then every 4th row 13 (8, 9, 0) times, every 6th row 0 (5, 6, 17) times—35 (39, 41, 43) sts. Work even until sleeve measures 6 (6¾, 7½, 10)"/15 (17, 19, 25.5)cm from pick up. Bind off in pat.

COLLAR

With WS facing, pick up and k22 (23, 23, 24) sts along left front neck edge, k 31 (33, 33, 35) sts from back neck holder, pick up and k22 (23, 23, 24) sts along right front—75 (79, 79, 83) sts. Work in Seed st for 1¾ (2¼, 2½, 3)"/4.5 (5.5, 6.5, 7.5)cm. Bind off in pat.

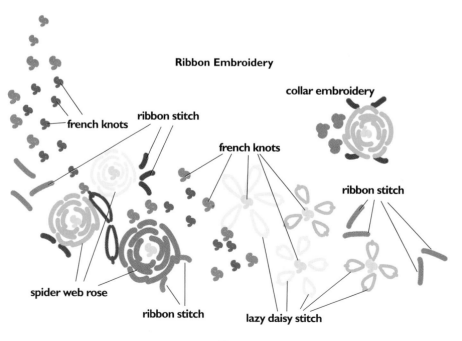

Ribbon Embroidery

collar embroidery

ribbon stitch

french knots

french knots

ribbon stitch

spider web rose

ribbon stitch

lazy daisy stitch

Buttonband

With RS facing, pick up and k 55 (59, 65, 79) sts along left front straight edge (omitting collar). Work in seed st for 7 rows. Bind off in pat. Place markers for 5 (5, 6, 7) buttons with the first and last ones ½"/1.5cm from upper and lower edges and rem 3 (3, 4, 5) spaced evenly between.

Buttonhole band

With RS facing, pick up and k 55 (59, 65, 79) sts evenly along right front to beg of collar. Work in seed st for 3 rows. **Next row (RS)** Work buttonholes opposite markers as foll: k2tog, yo. Work 3 more rows. Bind off in pat.

Sew side and sleeve seams. Sew on buttons.

EMBROIDERY

Work floral embroidery at fronts and collar edges. Use diagram and photo as a guide.

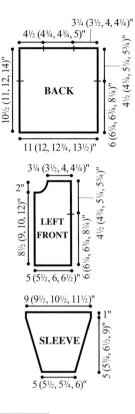

BACK

10½ (11, 12, 14)"

11 (12, 12¾, 13½)"

4½ (4¾, 4¾, 5)"

3¼ (3½, 4, 4¼)"

6 (6¼, 6¾, 8¼)"

4½ (4¾, 5¼, 5¾)"

LEFT FRONT

2"

8½ (9, 10, 12)"

5 (5½, 6, 6½)"

3¼ (3½, 4, 4¼)"

6 (6¼, 6¾, 8¼)"

4½ (4¾, 5¼, 5¾)"

SLEEVE

9 (9½, 10½, 11½)"

5 (5½, 5¾, 6)"

1"

5 (5¾, 6½, 9)"

Two adorable, intarsia-knit puppies adorn the front of this carry-all. Lined with iron-on interfacing, it is enough to hold all of your tot's necessities. Designed by Amy Bahrt.

KNITTED MEASUREMENTS

▓ 12" x 16" x 3"/30.5cm x 40.5cm x 7.5cm

MATERIALS

▓ 5 1¾oz/50g balls (each approx 74yd/ 68m) of Tahki Yarn/Tahki•Stacy Charles Inc. *Cotton Classic II* (cotton④) in #2856 navy (A),

▓ 3 balls in #2488 red (B)

▓ 1 ball each in #2744 green (C), #2003 ecru (D), and #2002 black (E)

▓ Size 7 (4.5mm) needles *or size to obtain gauge*

▓ 1yd/1m heavy iron-on interfacing

▓ 1yd/1m lining fabric (optional)

▓ 2 dog bone buttons: 1 off-white, 1 black, approx 1⅜"/35mm

▓ Bobbins

GAUGE

18 sts and 24 rows to 4"/10cm over St st using size 7 (4.5mm) needles.
Take time to check gauge .

Note

When changing colors, twist yarns on WS to prevent holes in work. Use a separate bobbin of yarn for each large block of color. If desired, small diamonds on argyle pat can be embroidered in duplicate st after piece is knit.

BAG

With A, beg at top of back piece, cast on 71 sts and work in St st for 2"/5cm, end with RS row. K next row on WS for turning ridge. Cont in St st as foll: Work 8 rows A, 2 rows B, 8 rows C, 35 rows B, 1 row A. Work 17 rows of argyle chart. Work 1 row A. Piece should measure approx 14"/35.5cm from top edge. P next row on RS for turning ridge. Cont in St st for 3"/7.5cm, ending with a RS row. K next row on WS for turning ridge. Work 2 rows with A. Work 17 rows argyle chart. Work 1 row A, 2 rows B. Work 31 rows dog chart. Work 2 rows B, 8 rows C, 2 rows B, 8 rows A. With A, k next row on WS for turning ridge then cont in St st for 2"/5cm. Bind off on WS.

GUSSET

On 3"/7.5cm center part, with A, pick up and k 15 sts along side. Work in St st for approx 12"/30.5cm, end with a WS row. P next row on RS for turning ridge. Cont in St st for 2"/5cm. Bind off on WS.

STRAPS

With A, cast on 11 sts. Work in St st for approx 25"/63.5cm, or desired length. Bind off.

FINISHING

Cut iron interfacing to size and carefully press on the entire piece. Press interfacing on side panels (gusset). Press interfacing on both straps. Close seam on straps from outside and close ends (fold in half). Turn bag to WS and sew side seams with panels. Press facing along turning ridge line and whipstitch down. Sew lining with same dimensions as bag. Hand tack to facing. Attach straps 4"/10cm from side seams. Sew french knots for eyes as indicated on dog chart.

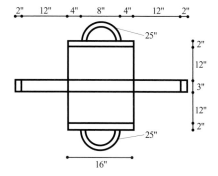

Color Key

■ Navy (A) ■ Green (C) ■ Black (E)

■ Red (B) □ Ecru (D) ● or ○ French knot

Argyle Chart

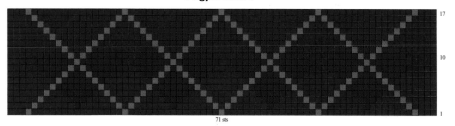

71 sts

Dog Chart

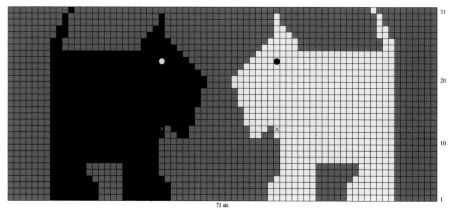

71 sts

VICTORIAN LAYETTE

Old-fashioned charm

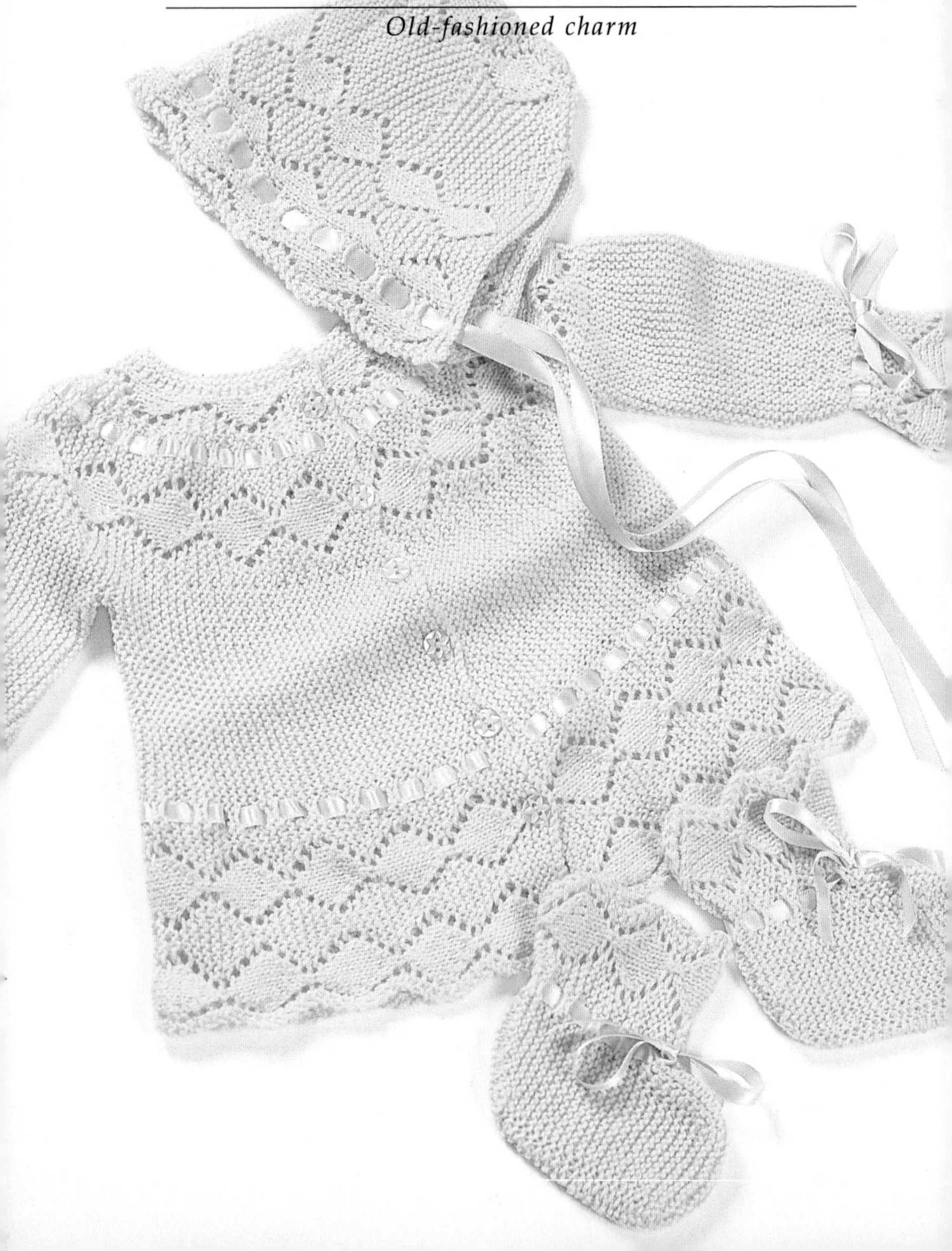

Margaret Stove, a master lace knitter, designed this delicate, diamond lace layette with a fine wool yarn. Silky ribbon threads through the eyelets for an elegant touch. It is sure to be passed along for generations to come.

To fit newborn to 3 months

KNITTED MEASUREMENTS
▨ Chest (buttoned) 17"/43cm
▨ Length 10½"/26.5cm
▨ Head circumference 12"/30.5cm

MATERIALS
▨ 4 1½oz/40g balls (each approx 165yd/150m) of Filatura Di Crosa/Tahki•Stacy Charles, Inc. *Monbébé* (wool①) in #504 pink
▨ One pair size 2 (2.5mm) needles *or size to obtain gauge*
▨ One size 2 (2.5mm) dpn
▨ Stitch holders
▨ 5yd/4.6m pink satin ribbon ¼"/6mm wide
▨ Seven ⅜"/10mm buttons

GAUGE
32 sts and 64 rows to 4"/10cm over garter st using size 2 (2.5mm) needles.
Take time to check gauge

STITCH GLOSSARY
Diamond Pattern
Row 1 (RS) K3, ssk, yo, k1, yo, k2tog, k3.

Rows 2 and 16 K5, p1, k5.
Row 3 K2, ssk, yo, k3, yo, k2tog, k2.
Rows 4 and 14 K4, p3, k4.
Row 5 K1, ssk, yo, k5, yo, k2tog, k1.
Rows 6 and 12 K3, p5, k3.
Row 7 Ssk, yo, k7, yo, k2tog.
Rows 8 and 10 K2, p7, k2.
Row 9 K1, yo, k2tog, k5, ssk, yo, k1.
Row 11 K2, yo, k2tog, k3, ssk, yo, k2.
Row 13 K3, yo, k2tog, k1, ssk, yo, k3.
Row 15 K4, yo, sl next 2 sts as if to k2tog, k1, pass 2 slipped sts over k1, yo, k4.
Rep rows 1-16 for diamond pat.

Lace Edging
Row 1 (RS) K1, ssk, yo, k1, yo, k2tog, k3.
Rows 2 and 16 K5, p1, k3.
Row 3 K2, yo, k3, yo, k2tog, k2.
Rows 4 and 14 K4, p3, k3.
Row 5 K2, yo, k5, yo, k2tog, k1.
Rows 6 and 12 K3, p5, k3.
Row 7 K2, yo, k7, yo, k2tog.
Rows 8 and 10 K,2 p7, k3.
Row 9 K2, yo, k2tog, k5, ssk, yo, k1.
Row 11 K1, ssk, yo, k2tog, k3, ssk, yo, k2.
Row 13 K1, ssk, yo, k2tog, k1, ssk, yo, k3.
Row 15 K3, yo, sl next 2 sts as if to k2tog, k1, pass 2 slipped sts over k1, yo, k4.
Rep rows 1-16 for lace edging.

Eyelet Pattern
Rows 1 and 2 Knit.
Row 3 (RS) K2tog, [yo] twice, ssk.
Row 4 K1, and k into front and back of double yo, k1.
Rep rows 1-4 for eyelet pat.

Note

Jacket is worked sideways, beg at left front and ending at right front.

JACKET

Cast on 72 sts loosely for left front edge and k 6 rows.

Beg pats and short row shaping

Row 1 Work lace edging over first 9 sts, work diamond pat over next 11 sts, work eyelet pat over next 4 sts, work garter st to last 22 sts. Turn. Cont in pats as established as foll: **Row 2** Sl 1, work to end. **Row 3** Work to last 22 sts, work diamond pat over next 11 sts, work eyelet pat over next 4 sts, turn. **Row 4** Sl 1, work to end. **Row 5** Rep row 3 until 4 sts of 2nd eyelet pat has been worked, k3, ssk, yo, k2. These last 7 sts make a half diamond pat at neck edge. The half diamond is the first 6 sts for the RS and the last 6 sts for the WS of the diamond pat plus a 1-st garter st edge. **Row 6** K1, p1, k5, work to end. Cont short row shaping by repeating the last 6 rows until 71 shaping rows have been worked, end at neck edge.

LEFT SLEEVE

Work first 28 sts, leave rem sts on a spare needle or holder. Cast on 43 sts loosely at the yoke edge for left sleeve.

Row 1 (cuff edge) Work lace edging over 9 sts, eyelet pat over 4 sts, work garter st to last 22 sts, turn.

Row 2 Sl 1 and knit to last 13 sts, turn.

Row 3 Sl 1 and knit sleeve sts to yoke,

then cont shaping yoke as before. Work the next 3 rows across all the cuff sts, keeping the eyelet and border pattern as established and the yoke shaping as before. Cont working yoke and cuff with short rows until 64 rows of the diamond border have been worked on the cuff, end at cuff edge. Using dpn, pick up 43 sts from the cast-on edge of sleeve and k tog one st from each needle, binding off the the underarm sts to make the sleeve seam. Without breaking the yarn, complete row across sts on holder.

Cont pats as established, shaping yoke as for front, until 143 rows of border pat have been completed. Work second sleeve as for first sleeve. Complete the front by working a further 72 shaping rows. Work 2 rows in garter st, then make the button holes as foll: K14, [yo, k2tog, k9] 5 times, yo, k2tog, k to end. Work 2 more rows in garter st, then bind off all sts loosely.

Neckband

With RS facing, pick up and knit 89 sts arounf neck edge. Work 3 rows in garter st. **Next row (RS)** K1, k2tog, yo, k to end. Bind off loosely.

FINISHING

Thread ribbon through eyelet holes at yoke and lower border. Sew on buttons.

BOOTIES

Cast on 27 sts loosely.

Row 1 Work lace edging over first 9 sts, work in garter st to last st, k into front and back of last st.

Row 2 Work in pats as established.

Row 3 Cont lace edging, then work eyelet pat over next 4 sts (these sts form leg of bootie), k7, turn.

Rows 4, 6, 8 and 10 Sl 1, work to end.

Row 5 Work leg sts, k9, turn.

Row 7 Work leg sts, k11, turn.

Row 9 Work leg sts, k13, turn.

Row 11 Work leg sts, k to end. Work even over all sts until row 15 of second diamond has been completed.

Next row (WS) K15, turn. Cont in garter st on these 15 sts for 15 more rows.

Next row K15, return to pat sts and pick up 8 loops (every second row of garter st) along the adjacent straight edge, then turn work back to WS and knit the 8 sts followed by the leg sts to end.

INSTEP

Rows 1 and 7 Work leg, k to end.

Row 2 K to leg sts, work to end.

Rows 3 and 11 Work leg sts, k to last 2 sts, turn.

Rows 4, 6, 8 and 10 Sl 1, k to leg sts, work to end.

Rows 5 and 9 Work leg sts, k to last 4 sts, turn. Pick up 21 loops along lower sole edge.

Row 12 Sl 1, knit to leg sts, work to end.

Rows 13 and 15 Work leg sts, k to st before picked up sts and k last st with picked-up st. Turn.

Row 14 Sl 1, k to leg sts, work to end.

Row 16 Sl 1, k13, k2tog, turn. Rep row 16 thirteen times more.

Next row Sl 1, k13, k2tog, cont across leg sts. Rep rows 13 and 14 eleven times.

Shape heel

Row 1 Work leg sts, k13, turn.

Rows 2, 4, 6 and 8 Sl 1, k to leg sts, work to end.

Row 3 Work leg sts, k11, turn.

Row 5 Work leg sts, k9, turn.

Row 7 Work leg sts, k7, turn.

Row 9 Work leg, k14, k2tog.

Row 10 K2tog, k13, work leg sts. Join back seam of bootie by picking up a loop for each st of cast-on edge. Graft or place right sides tog and then sl st from front needle to back needle. Slide RH needle through slipped st and bring next st through at the same time, taking first slipped st off needle. Bring the st from back needle to front needle and rep as for first st. Cont in this way until all sts have been worked off needles. Fasten off and darn in ends. Thread ribbon through eyelets at ankle and tie.

CAP

Cast on 44 sts.

Row 1 Work edge pat on first 9 sts, diamond pat on next 11 sts and use the next 4 sts for the eyelet pat, k14, ssk, yo, k1, yo, k2tog, k1.

Row 2 K3, p1, k16, work to end.

Row 3 Work border, k13, ssk, yo, k3, yo, k2.

Row 4 K3, p3, k15, work to end.

Row 5 Work border , k12, ssk, yo, k5, yo, k2.

Row 6 K3, p5, k14, work to end.

Row 7 Work border, k11, ssk, yo, k7, yo, k2.

Row 8 Sl 1, k2, p7, k13, work to end.

Row 9 Work border, k12, yo, k2tog, k5, ssk, yo, k2. Pick up 1 st at end of 2nd, 4th and 6th rows.

Row 10 Sl 1, k2, p5, k13, work to end.

Row 11 Work border, k13, yo, k2tog, k3, ssk, k2tog, k2tog (last st with pick-up loop), turn.

Row 12 Sl 1, k2, k5, k14, work to end.

Row 13 Work border, k14, yo, k2tog, k1, ssk, yo, [k2tog] twice, turn.

Row 14 Sl 1, k2, p3, k15, work to end.

Row 15 Work border, k15, yo sl 2 sts as if to k2tog, k1, pass 2 slipped sts overy k1, yo, [k2tog] twice, turn.

Row 16 Sl 1, k2, p1, k16, work to end.

Row 17 Work border, k to last 4 sts, turn.

Row 18 Sl 1, k15, work to end.

Row 19 Cont working 2 sts fewer at crown end on RS rows until 2nd diamond of border is complete (32 rows). Rep rows 1 to 32 four times more. Join back seam as for booties or graft edges tog. Thread ribbon through eyelet holes and make bow to finish.

BONNET

Cast on 45 sts

Row 1 Work edge pat over first 4 sts, (k1, ssk, yo, k1), k4 sts for eyelet pat and complete edge pat, beg with k1 (ie: k1, yo, k2tog, k3), then work diamond pat on next 11 sts, k14, ssk, yo, k1, yo, k2tog, k1.

Row 2 K3, p1, k16, work to end.

Row 3 Work border, k13, ssk, yo, k3, yo, k2.

Row 4 K3, p3, k15, work to end.

Row 5 Work border, k12, ssk, yo, k5, yo, k2.

Row 6 K3, p5, k14, work to end.

Row 7 Work border, k11, ssk, yo, k7, yo, k2.

Row 8 Sl 1, k2, p7, k13, work to end.

Row 9 Work border, k12, yo, k2tog, k5, ssk, yo k2. Pick up 1 st at end of 2nd, 4th and 6th rows.

Row 10 Sl 1, k2, p5, k13, work to end.

Row 11 Work border, k13, yo, k2tog, k3, ssk, k2tog, k2tog (last st with picked up loop), turn.

Row 12 Sl 1, k2, k5, k14, work to end.

Row 13 Work border, k14, yo, k2tog, k1, ssk, yo, [k2tog] twice, turn.

Row 14 Sl 1, k2, p3, k15, work to end.

Row 15 Work border, k15, yo, sl 2 as if to k2tog, k1, pass 2 slipped sts over k1, yo, [k2tog] twice, turn.

Row 16 Sl 1, k2, p1, k16, work to end.

Row 17 Work border, k to last 4 sts, turn.

Row 18 Sl 1, k15, work to end.

Row 19 Cont working 2 sts fewer at crown on RS rows until 2nd diamond of border is complete (32 rows). Rep rows 1 to 32 four times more. Join back seam as for booties or graft edges tog to four short row turns past center diamond. Pick up and k 68 sts along neck edge of each side of bonnet. K 3 rows. Bind off. Darn in ends. Thread ribbon through eyelet holes and secure at neck edge. Leave sufficient ribbon to tie.

NOTES

RESOURCES

US RESOURCES

Write to the yarn companies listed below for purchasing and mail-order information.

AURORA YARNS
PO Box 3068
Moss Beach, CA 94038-3068

BERROCO, INC.
14 Elmdale Rd.
PO Box 367
Uxbridge, MA 01569

CHERRY TREE HILL YARN
PO Box 659
Barton, VT 05822

CLASSIC ELITE YARNS
300A Jackson Street
Bldg. 5
Lowell, MA 01852

CLECKHEATON
distributed by
Plymouth Yarn

DALE OF NORWAY, INC.
N16 W23390 Stoneridge Drive
Suite A
Waukesha, WI 53188

FILATURA DI CROSA
distributed by
Tahki•Stacy Charles, Inc.

FILANDER
distributed by
Trendsetter Yarns

GARNSTUDIO
distributed by
Aurora Yarns

GRIGNASCO
distributed by
JCA

JO SHARP
distributed by
Classic Elite Yarns

JCA
35 Scales Lane
Townsend, MA 01469

KIC2, LLC
2220 Eastman Ave. #105
Ventura, CA 93003

LANG
distributed by
Berroco, Inc.

LANE BORGOSESIA
PO Box 217
Colorado Springs, CO 80903

LION BRAND YARN CO.
34 West 15th Street
New York, NY 10011

NATURALLY
distributed
S. R. Kertzer, Ltd.

PLYMOUTH YARN
PO Box 28
Bristol, PA 19007

REYNOLDS
distributed by
JCA

ROWAN YARNS
5 Northern Blvd.
Amherst, NH 03031

SESIA
distributed by
Lane Borgosesia

S. R. KERTZER, LTD.
105A Winges Road
Woodbridge, ON L4L 6C2
Canada

TAHKI•STACY CHARLES, INC.
1059 Manhattan Ave.
Brooklyn, NY 11222

TAHKI YARNS
distributed by
Tahki•Stacy Charles, Inc.

TRENDSETTER YARNS
16742 Stagg Street
Suite 104
Van Nuys, CA 91406

CANADIAN RESOURCES

Write to US resources for mail-order availability of yarns not listed.

AURORA YARNS
PO Box 28553
Aurora, ON L4G 6S6

BERROCO, INC.
distributed by
S. R. Kertzer, Ltd.

CLASSIC ELITE YARNS
distributed by
S. R. Kertzer, Ltd.

CLECKHEATON
distributed by
Diamond Yarn

DIAMOND YARN
9697 St. Laurent
Montreal, PQ H3L 2N1
and
155 Martin Ross, Unit #3
Toronto, ON M3J 2L9

ESTELLE DESIGNS & SALES, LTD.
Units 65/67
2220 Midland Ave.
Scarborough, ON M1P 3E6

FILATURA DI CROSA
distributed by
Diamond Yarn

GARNSTUDIO
distributed by
Aurora Yarns

GRIGNASCO
distributed by
Estelle Designs & Sales, Ltd.

LANG
distributed by
Diamond Yarn

NATURALLY
distributed by
S. R. Kertzer, Ltd.

PATONS®
PO Box 40
Listowel, ON N4W 3H3

ROWAN
distributed by
Diamond Yarn

S. R. KERTZER, LTD.
105A Winges Rd.
Woodbridge, ON L4L 6C2

UK RESOURCES

Not all yarns used in this book are available in the UK. For yarns not available, make a comparable substitute or contact the US manufacturer for purchasing and mail-order information.

ROWAN YARNS
Green Lane Mill
Holmfirth
West Yorks HD7 1RW
Tel: 01484-681881

SILKSTONE
12 Market Place
Cockermouth
Cumbria CA13 9NQ
Tel: 01900-821052

THOMAS RAMSDEN GROUP
Netherfield Road
Guiseley
West Yorks LS20 9PD
Tel: 01943-872264

VOGUE KNITTING BABY GIFTS

Editor-in-Chief
TRISHA MALCOLM

Art Director
CHRISTINE LIPERT

Executive Editor
CARLA S. SCOTT

Managing Editor
SUZIE ELLIOTT

Contributing Editor
DARYL BROWER

Instruction Writer
MARI LYNN PATRICK

Technical Illustration Editor/
Page Layout
CHI LING MOY

Instructions Editor
KAREN GREENWALD

Instructions Coordinator
CHARLOTTE PARRY

Knitting Coordinator
JEAN GUIRGUIS

Yarn Coordinator
VERONICA MANNO

Editorial Coordinators
KATHLEEN KELLY
MICHELLE LO

Photography
BRIAN KRAUS, NYC
BOBB CONNORS
TERRANCE CARNEY
Photographed at Butterick Studios

Stylists
MONICA GAIGE-ROSENSWEIG
MELISSA MARTIN

Production Managers
LILLIAN ESPOSITO
WINNIE HINISH

President and CEO, Butterick® Company, Inc.
JAY H. STEIN

Executive Vice President and Publisher, Butterick® Company, Inc.
ART JOINNIDES